HODDER
English
Gold

1

Sue Hackman
Alan Howe

Hodder & Stoughton

A MEMBER OF THE HODDER HEADLINE GROUP

ACKNOWLEDGEMENTS

The publishers would like to thank the following contributors:

Sue Hackman   –   Unit One, *Quest*
Ken Kimber   –   Unit Two, *The Village*
Judith Langley   –   Unit Three, *Poetry Alive*
Darren Phillips   –   Unit Four, *The Language Investigators*
Cristina Bennett   –   Unit Five, *Storytelling*
Karen Blake and Lynette Newman   –   Unit Six, *Autobiography*

Copyright Text:
p52 from Earth Matters, Issue 34, © 1997 Friends of the Earth; pp120 and 122 from Sir Gawain and the Green Knight, as read by Hugh Lupton, Midwinter Tales audio cassette (audio cassettes available from The Company of Storytellers, 8 Church Terrace, Aylsham, Norfolk); p139 My Autobiography, Ian Botham © HarperCollins Publishers Ltd; pp140 and 152 My Life as a Woman, Roseanne Barr © HarperCollins Publishers Ltd; p152 My Left Foot, Christy Brown © Martin Secker & Warburg.

Copyright Photographs:
p40 [top] © Zefa, [middle] © Brenda Prince/Format, [bottom] © David Kampfner/Life File; p41 [top] © Mike Evans/Life File, [middle] © Nicola Sutton/Life File, [bottom] © Eddie Tan/ Life File; p61 © Action Plus; p66 © The Bridgeman Art Library; p67 © Bruce Coleman Ltd; p71 [left] 'October Sail (Yacht on the Medway opposite Gillingham)' by Vic Trevett © The Bridgeman Art Library, [right] 'The Bell Rock Lighthouse' by J.M.W. Turner by kind permission of the National Gallery of Scotland © Bruce Coleman Ltd; p74 [left, middle and right] © Bruce Coleman Ltd; p153 [clockwise from left] © Camerapress, © Corbis, © Andrew Hasson/Camerapress, © Linda R. Chen/Hollywood Pictures (courtesy of the Kobal Collection).

Every effort has been made to trace copyright holders of material reproduced in this book. Any rights not acknowledged here will be acknowledged in subsequent printings if notice is given to the publisher.

Orders: please contact Bookpoint Ltd, 39 Milton Park, Abingdon, Oxon OX14 4TD.
Telephone: (44) 01235 400414, Fax: (44) 01235 400454. Lines are open from 9.00 – 6.00,
Monday to Saturday, with a 24 hour message answering service. Email address: orders@bookpoint.co.uk

British Library Cataloguing in Publication Data
A catalogue record for this title is available from The British Library

ISBN 0 340 70181 1

First published 1998
Impression number 10 9 8 7 6 5
Year   2002 2001 2000

Copyright © 1998 Sue Hackman and Alan Howe

Designed and typeset by Mind's Eye Design, Lewes.

Printed in Dubai for Hodder & Stoughton Educational, a division of Hodder Headline Plc, 338 Euston Road, London NW1 3BH by Oriental Press

INTRODUCTION

Welcome to *Hodder English Gold*. This course book and its two companions represent a quality English curriculum for pupils working at levels 2–4 in Key Stage 3 (S1–3). It has been planned and written to meet the demands of the National Curriculum (and Scottish 5–14 Guidelines) and to maintain a challenging, vigorous and progressive ethos in the classroom. *Hodder English Gold 1* introduces pupils to a wide and challenging variety of English experiences and assignments which are then progressively built on and broadened in *Hodder English Gold 2* and *3*. However, teachers may wish to use these books to supplement their own schemes of work, or other materials.

RAISING STANDARDS AND COVERING NATIONAL CURRICULUM REQUIREMENTS

We have taken as our prime directive the advancement of pupil learning. All the materials in *Hodder English Gold* have been trialled in the classroom by English teachers to offer the very best of current practice. Units have been developed to cover the National Curriculum in England, Wales and Northern Ireland and the 5–14 Guidelines in Scotland. At the same time, we know that pupils in the early levels of literacy need explicit instruction and scaffolded activities. We have provided both in the context of purposeful work and quality texts. Each book contains one unit of work which addresses basic skills as a focus of work in its own right and consolidation activities have been built in later.

Hodder English Gold addresses the appropriate number of set texts and includes many more. Pre-twentieth century literature is amply represented in both fiction and non-fiction. You will find here a catholic range of genres, tones and forms, but we have resisted simplified versions in favour of abridgement. We have made particular efforts to ensure that speaking and listening is fully represented in the series, not merely as incidental group talk but as a purposeful activity in its own right.

STRUCTURE

Hodder English Gold consists of three books, one for each year at Key Stage 3 (years S1–3 in Scotland) and a cassette. Each book is divided into six units, and each of these units represents a half-term's work. The units have been arranged across the three years to establish, revisit and consolidate key skills.

Although the units have been placed in an order which offers pupils a varied and progressive experience of English (for example, the 'Poetry Alive' unit in *Hodder English Gold 1* introduces key skills in poetry which are then picked up in later units), you can use the book in a flexible way, linking units with others or with texts you want to teach.

Whilst we have introduced basic skills directly through key units, and again in the context of others, we also assume that teachers will continue to support individual pupils by giving them feedback on their oral and written performance, and that spelling, punctuation and grammar will be part of this continuing work.

PROGRESSION

Hodder English Gold 1, 2 and *3* form an incremental programme of work with clear goals written with the expressed intention of raising standards in English. The course offers far more than a sequence of self-contained lessons or starting points because progression is built into each unit, between each book and across the course as a whole. Key elements of English are focused on once in each year, and incidentally as a part of other units.

ASSESSMENT

Assessment is an integral part of each unit. However, checklists, recording sheets and assessment grids are deliberately not included, as it is most likely that you have already developed a workable system. Teaching by units enables you to collect evidence of pupils' achievements periodically, and systematically, at the end of each unit. The book provides the pupils with focused tasks and explicit criteria for evaluating how well they are doing, and what they need to improve on. Each unit begins with a clear set of teaching aims and objectives, which will need to be talked through with pupils and revisited as the unit progresses. You will be able to plan the precise nature of your assessments against these aims and objectives. Pupils' own self-assessment is also vital: each unit ends with a page for review and self-assessment or extension activities.

ACTIVITIES

The initial material and activities of each unit are designed to introduce pupils to the focus for the sequence of work, and to engage their interest. There is then a series of tasks designed to help pupils to develop specific areas of knowledge, understanding and skill. Several pages are given to consolidating new knowledge or skills in context.

USING *HODDER ENGLISH GOLD*

Many of the units are free-standing and teachers will find them sufficiently flexible to introduce extra material or to extend their use beyond a half-term. Texts have been chosen for their quality and for their richness in classroom study, as well as for their accessibility, and relevance for the age group. Where it has been impractical to reproduce whole texts, we have produced extracts to support the close study of key passages.

In addition, the cassette provides support where it is most helpful. To promote reading skills, we recommend that pupils conduct close study activities using the text as well as the tape so that they can learn how to find particular words, phrases and information in the text. Where icon **A** appears (see below), either on its own or as icon **B** (see below), the text which is being studied is provided on the cassette as well.

In *Hodder English Gold 1* there are some stories in Unit Five, 'Storytelling', which are intended to be heard rather than read. Where this is the case, the text of these stories has been provided at the back of the book so that the teacher can tell the story if preferred.

For your convenience, a number of pages have been designed as *photocopiable*. These pages contain activities which pupils will do best if they are involved in hands-on work.

A   **B**

CONTENTS

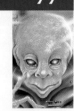

GUIDELINES FOR TEACHERS

UNIT ONE – QUEST

This unit is organised in stages to build up an extended narrative. You can create a good piece of coursework by collecting each item of work on a separate piece of paper to be bound together as an adventure scrapbook at the end.

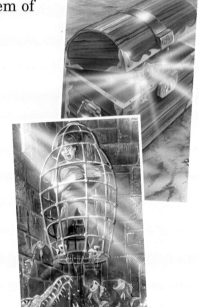

Teaching Points
The unit is designed to be very flexible in the way you teach it. It works best if the class moves through the stages together. This way you can control the pace of work to keep up the momentum and to linger when pupils' imaginations have been caught.

However, for confident pupils, the unit is sufficiently self-explanatory to allow them to move ahead at their own pace, and it would not be difficult for you or them to make up new challenges to include in the quest.

Note that the problem-solving and puzzle elements work best in small groups, and are good for engaging interest.

UNIT TWO – THE VILLAGE

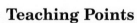

This unit is designed to introduce pupils to a range of drama conventions and techniques in the context of an imagined village community. Pupils are required to adopt a role as a villager and, in role, to develop their understanding of a range of issues affecting the community. In the process, pupils are guided through non-narrative reading and writing tasks.

Teaching Points
A key feature of this unit is the need for pupils to work in small groups. Towards the end of the unit there is a 'public meeting'

which requires pupils to voice their ideas and opinions in a more formal setting. Your teaching will need to highlight the skills required for both informal group work and to help pupils address the requirements of a more structured, formal nature.

The drama conventions that pupils will undertake and learn are: working in role; play-making; freeze frame; hot-seating; public meeting. All are clearly explained in the text.

As the unit features news reports and articles for pupils to both read and write about, it would be helpful if you could gather together a collection of articles on local or national issues of the day.

UNIT THREE – POETRY ALIVE

Unlike other units, this unit is organised as a sequence of sections each introducing a new aspect of poetry, and each one containing an example.

Teaching Points

Some of the poems will look challenging on first sight, but they have been double-checked in classroom use and

produce high levels of involvement and excellent work. For additional support, the poem in the section on onomatopeia is read aloud on the accompanying cassette. We have gone for poems that will appeal to pupils, read aloud well and suggest writing activities.

We recommend that you reserve time for the final section 'Writing about a Poem' because it is here that pupils have to synthesise what they have learnt about different techniques.

UNIT FOUR – LANGUAGE INVESTIGATORS

This is an important unit in the study of grammar, spelling and punctuation. The other books in the series, and other units in this book, build on it by revisiting its key points and consolidating them in use.

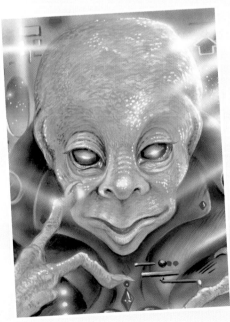

Teaching Points

We decided against including lists of answers in order to deter short-cuts. It is better to know if there are problems.

You will recognise lots of opportunities to branch into extra examples if pupils show an interest in word history, or if you want to extend the work on prefixes, suffixes and grammar or even applying the spelling strategies to pupils' own lists of tricky words.

UNIT FIVE – STORYTELLING

The main focus of this unit is narrative, both written and spoken. Pupils are introduced to the key features of *oral* narrative and guided through a range of tasks designed to develop their understanding and skill as storytellers.

Teaching Points

Pupils' learning and enjoyment will be considerably advanced by use of the accompanying cassette. This contains a variety of oral narratives, including a short anecdote told by a Year 7 pupil and extracts from traditional tales. Pupils will gain immensely from repeated listening to these taped stories. However, for the purposes of the tasks on pp106, 109, 126 and 128, the texts are provided on pp157 to 160 for you to tell the stories if you prefer.

In addition to the material in the unit, try to gather together a collection of suitable traditional tales so that pupils can extend their experience of this form of narrative. If you can learn a tale or two yourself, and *tell* them (rather than read them) to your class, this will considerably enhance the unit.

You will need to think about how to organise your classroom so that pupils can work in pairs and small groups, as well as form an audience when they are telling their own stories.

Writing tasks are carefully structured to help pupils build up their understanding of story structure and patterns in narrative, and there are plenty of opportunities for focused language study – adjectives, nouns, verbs and adverbs. Ultimately, however, the unit is designed to increase pupils' confidence and skill in sequencing a coherent narrative, with lots of practical examples: enjoyment should be a central ingredient!

UNIT SIX – AUTOBIOGRAPHY

This unit asks pupils to read and respond to a range of extracts from recently published autobiographies, and to use the knowledge they gain to build up material for a short autobiography of their own. This kind of activity often features as the *first* unit in a scheme of work: here it is deliberately situated at the *end* of the first year's work so that pupils can build on skills they have been developing as readers, writers, speakers and listeners in previous units. The unit is carefully structured so that pupils can build up a portfolio of pieces which eventually will form a substantial piece of written work. However, a key outcome of the unit is also a spoken task, in which pupils interview each other about their lives as part of a simulated chat-show.

Teaching Points

Many pupils will need support and guidance in order to be able to complete the opening sections where they are asked to read a range of extracts from published autobiographies. These are available on the accompanying cassette.

The writing tasks are designed to be lively and engaging, and pupils should be encouraged to attempt these for themselves in draft first. Many will profit from appropriate support in improving their writing for final presentation. There are opportunities for good use of IT at this point.

You might wish to end the year on a high note by encouraging pupils to make book covers and display their finished autobiographies in class or the school library, and/or invite parents to a 'book launch'.

Quest

A quest is a journey in search of something which has been lost. It is also an adventure. In this unit you will go on a quest. You will write about your adventure in several stages. You will develop your skills as:

SPEAKERS AND LISTENERS

by talking about the choices you make in your adventure

by discussing your work with others

READERS

by following instructions

by answering questions about things you read

WRITERS

by describing what you see and do on your adventure

by writing a poem

by writing a set of instructions

Now turn the page to begin your quest...

THE CROWN

Imagine a box. Inside the box is a crown.

- Imagine the crown. Draw it, but don't show anyone.

- Write a description of the crown. Use these words to help you:

    gold jewels shining rubies
    glitter light sparkle colour

- Swap your description with someone else. Ask them to draw the crown just as you describe it. In return, you draw theirs.

- Did they draw what you described? Add or change your description to make it easier for the reader to see.

THE PURPOSE OF YOUR QUEST

You have received this urgent letter. It has been damaged.
Study the letter and work out what it said.

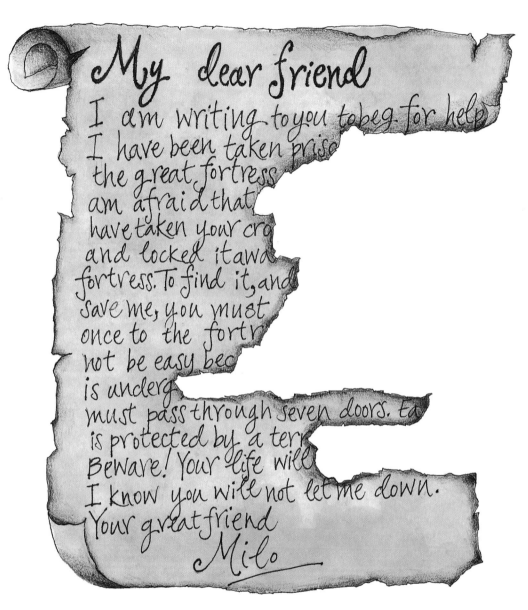

My dear friend
I am writing to you to beg for help
I have been taken priso
the great fortress
am afraid that
have taken your cro
and locked it awa
fortress. To find it, and
save me, you must
once to the fortr
not be easy bec
is underg
must pass through seven doors. Ea
is protected by a terr
Beware! Your life will
I know you will not let me down.
Your great friend
Milo

• Work out what the letter said and, on a separate
  sheet, fill in the missing words.

• Discuss the following questions in groups.

  1 What has happened to Milo?

  2 What has happened to the box?

  3 What does Milo want you to do?

HELPERS

To rescue Milo and the crown, you can choose two helpers.
Your helpers will be useful later in the quest. They will help
you out of danger.

- Give names to your helpers.
- Give them one special power each.
- Complete two character passports for each helper. An example
  of a passport is given above.

HELP

- Your helpers can come from other planets or imaginary countries.
- They can have unusual personalities.

KIT

Your journey is long and you must travel light. You can only carry six things between you.

- In groups of three, discuss what you should take with you. Here are some ideas. Choose two things from each list.

List 1	**List 2**	**List 3**
An axe	A blanket	A first aid kit
A blow-up raft	A book about survival	A grappling hook
A water flask	A rope	A telescope
Slippers	Chocolate	Sponge bag with soap and toothbrush
A folding knife with extra blades	Matches	A change of clothes
A hammock	A walkman (with batteries)	The complete works of Shakespeare

- On a separate sheet, write down your six items. Next to each one write down why you think it will be valuable to you. Set your work out like this:

Item	*Reason*
Water Flask	*We may get thirsty on the quest.*

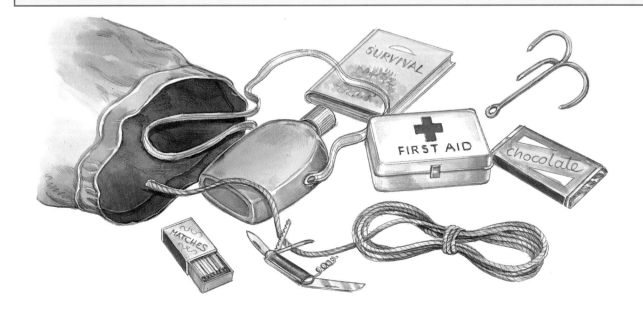

THE FORTRESS

The crown and your friend Milo are locked in the middle of a huge underground fortress. To reach the fortress you must travel through a tunnel. It is blocked at various stages by doors. The illustration below shows these stages.

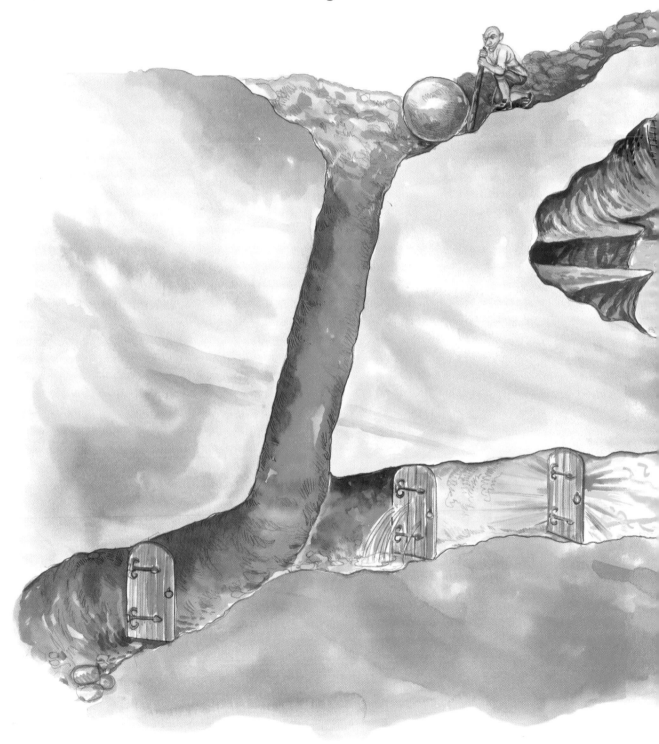

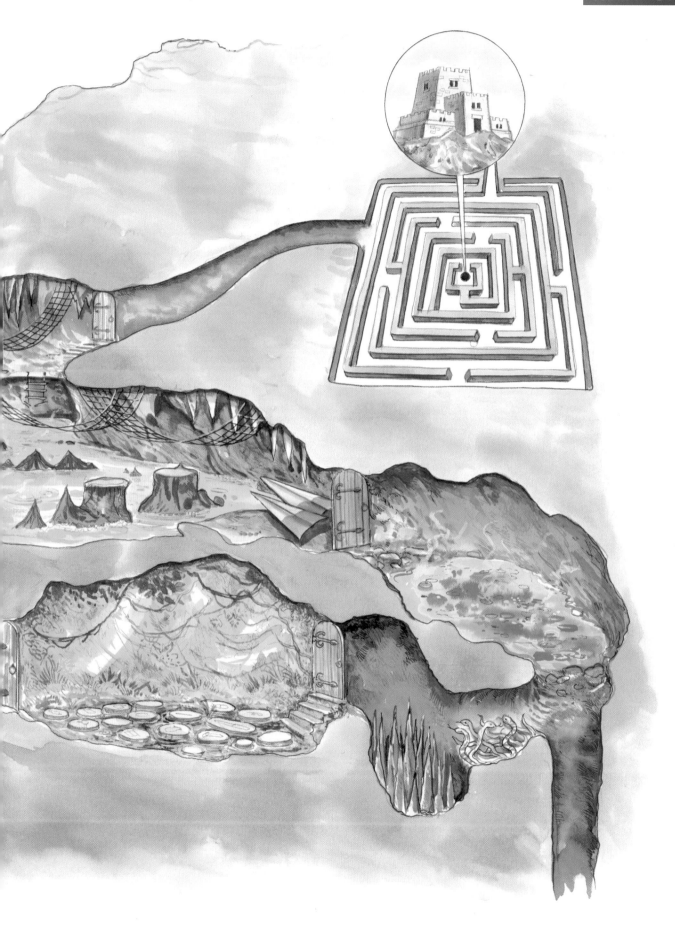

THE BEAST

The entrance to the tunnel is protected by The Beast.

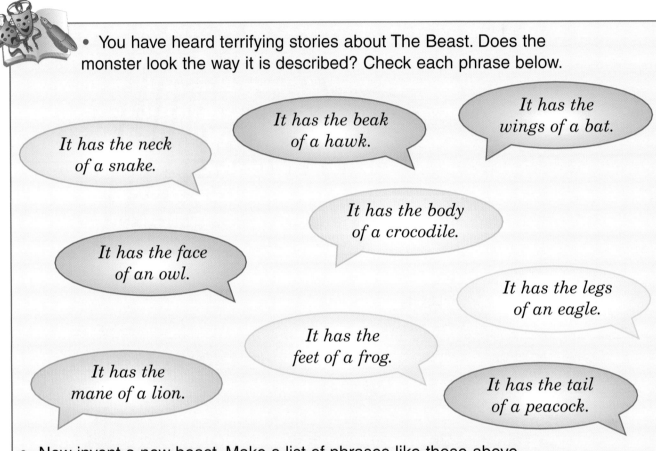

- • You have heard terrifying stories about The Beast. Does the monster look the way it is described? Check each phrase below.

It has the neck of a snake.

It has the beak of a hawk.

It has the wings of a bat.

It has the body of a crocodile.

It has the face of an owl.

It has the legs of an eagle.

It has the feet of a frog.

It has the mane of a lion.

It has the tail of a peacock.

- • Now invent a new beast. Make a list of phrases like those above. Ask a partner to use your list to draw it. In return, you draw theirs.

- • How will you get past The Beast? Will there be a fight? Or will you use a trick or a special power? Write a paragraph about the way you beat the beast. You can use these starters to help you or you can make up your own.

  1 When I first saw the beast, I felt…
  2 I could see it clearly now. It was…
  3 I had to act quickly, so I…
  4 The beast saw me and…
  5 There was risky moment when…
  6 Luckily, I…
  7 I realised we had won when…
  8 As we slipped past, I thought…

THE FIRST DOOR

Standing by the first door, you can hear a rumbling sound which grows louder and louder. The ground begins to shake and the door begins to rattle.

You put your eye to the keyhole and see an enormous ball of stone rolling towards you. This boulder crushes everything in its path.

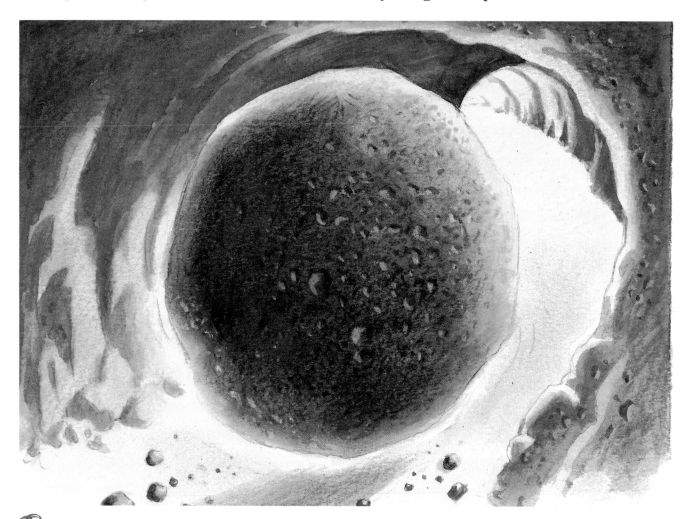

- How will you get past the boulder to the next door? Talk about your ideas with a partner.

- On your own, write one paragraph which describes how you escaped from the boulder. Use the title:

  How We Got Past the Boulder.

- Did you use any of your helpers' special powers? Did you use something from your kit?

- Finish your paragraph by arriving outside the second door, but do not enter it yet.

THE WEEPING DOOR

You find yourself outside the second door. Just as you are about to open it, you notice water seeping from the gaps between the door and the wall.

- Why might there be water oozing out?
  What are the risks of opening the door?
  What will you do if the worst happens?
  How can you use your helpers? Discuss with a partner what you will do.

- Now describe what happens. Use the title: *The Weeping Door.*
  Start your writing like this:

  1 We could see water seeping from the second door.

  2 After a moment, I decided to…

  3 And secondly, I thought…

  4 There was a risk that…

  5 We prepared ourselves by…

  6 I turned the handle and…

- Now continue your writing, up to where you arrive at the third door.

THE DOOR OF COLOURS

The door to the next stage of your quest is alight with colour.
From every crack pours a ray of light, each a different colour.

- There is a spell to open the door. It is a description of the colours. Unfortunately, you are forbidden to use their actual names. Instead, you must find a way to describe them. For example:

THE SPELL

My first is the colour of rubies and blood

My second is the colour of earth and wood

My third is the colour of sea and sky

My fourth is the colour of darkest night

My fifth is …

- What are the first four colours? Colour them in on a photocopy of the drawing of the door opposite.

- Colour in the other rays in your own choice of colours.

- Complete the spell for the door you have drawn. The lines must rhyme in pairs (see the Help Box below).

- Finish the spell with two lines commanding the door to open.

HELP

Rhyme

Words that rhyme end with the same sound. For example:

Slow and go

Log and dog

Sink and think

Chew and do

Rice and nice

Think of rhymes for:

Sack

Bone

Rat

Take

Blood

Many poets write poems that rhyme.

THE CORRIDOR OF COLOURS

When you open this third door, you
start the best part of your adventure.
There are no monsters here, just a
wonderful display of lights all around
you as you walk through the tunnel to
the next door.

• Describe your wonderful experience. Write down

    what you see

    what you feel

    what you hear

    what you think

Begin your writing like this:

As soon as I opened the third door, I saw...

THE PUZZLE

All good things must come to an end. You arrive at the fourth door and on it you see this sign:

BEWARE!
DO NOT ENTER!
The ground is dangerous
One touch means instant death!

The stepping-stones are booby traps!
Only one way is safe!

TURN BACK NOW!

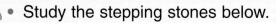

- Study the stepping stones below.

- Can you solve the puzzle and work out the safe stepping stones to get you to the next door?

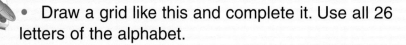

- Draw a grid like this and complete it. Use all 26 letters of the alphabet.

Alphabet	A word that begins with this letter	A word that has this letter in the middle	A word that ends with this letter
A	apple	bat	spa
B	bug	abbey	crab
C			

- Are there any letters of the alphabet which are not found at the beginning of words?

- Are there any letters of the alphabet which are not found in the middle of words?

- Are there any letters of the alphabet which are not found at the end of words?

THE TERRIBLE TUNNEL

The fifth door opens easily. This stage of the tunnel is very dangerous! Look at the map below and think how you will get to the next door.

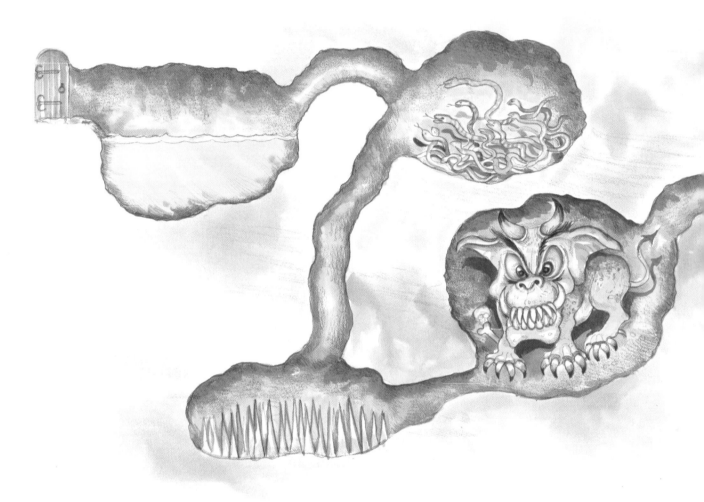

- • Can you use any of your helpers' special powers?
- • Can you use any of the things you carry with you?
- • Work out a plan with your imaginary helpers. Write down what you say to them. Look at the Help Box opposite to find out how to write down what you say.

Start your writing like this:

"Okay, I think I know how we're going to do this! Here is the plan. First..."

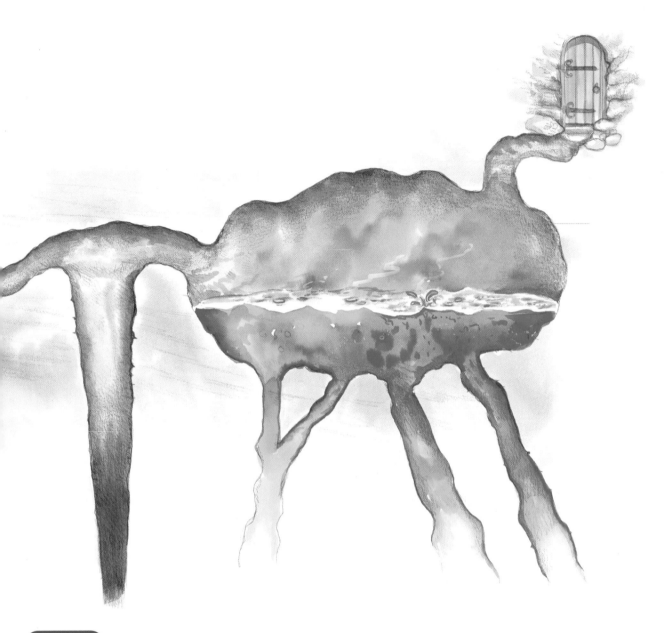

SPEECH MARKS

1 Put speech marks around the words you say.

2 Put a comma between the spoken bit and the rest of the sentence (for example, before *he said*).

3 Start a new line when someone new starts to speak.

For example:

"Friends, I think I have an idea," I said.

"I hope it's a good idea," replied Zeptor, "because I can't see how we will make it to the next door."

HANG, GLIDE AND FLY

You come out of the tunnel through door six. You find yourself on a ledge. Below you is an acid lake. You have to get to the next door without touching the ground.

In front of you are three gliders. Above you is a system of nets and ropes.

- How can you use the gliders, nets and ropes to get across the acid lake?

- Write down the stages of your journey without using the words:

go   going   went

get   getting   got

use   using   used

HELP

Over-used words

The point of this exercise is to find alternatives to over-used words.

Go, Going and Went
For go, going and went, try describing the way you moved, for example:

swung, leaped.

Get, Getting and Got
See if you can cut out get, getting and got by changing the word that comes after it. For example:

got hold of → *holding*
he got hurt → *he hurt himself*

Or you can try a new word:

got on → *climbed on*
got off → *jumped off*

Use, Using and Used
Find different words for use, using and used by thinking about *how* you used things to get across. For example:

I used the glider to get to →
I grabbed the glider and I flew to

Other over-used words
Other over-used words include:

nice good said big

Look up these words in a thesaurus or dictionary. Make a list of alternative words for each one.

THE MAZE

When you enter the final door (door seven), you see a maze
ahead of you. The fortress is in the middle of the maze.

- Look at the illustration. Write down the directions
  through the maze so that others can follow.

HELP

Giving instructions

Good instructions:

- Are brief, simple and easy to follow

- Direct the reader left or right

- Mention landmarks, for example:

  Turn left at the red triangle

- Give the number of the turning, for
  example, second left

Check if your instructions are clear by
asking someone else to find their way
using them.

entrance

RESCUE

You have made it to the fortress! Inside, you find your friend Milo locked in a cage. Milo is holding the box containing the crown. The cage is hanging by a rope above a pool of piranhas and alligators.

- Look at the illustration. Working with a partner, plan your rescue of both Milo and the crown.

1 Are you going to use any of your helpers' special powers?

2 What will your helpers do?

3 Can you use an item from your kit?

- On your own, write a description of the rescue. How is your quest going to end?

WHAT DID YOU LEARN?

You have successfully completed the quest.

Ask yourself how much you have learnt from this unit.

Answer the questions below:

1 When you describe an object, what sort of information helps to give a clear picture?

2 What is a rhyme? Give examples of rhymes to king, toy and chew.

3 Name three over-used words. Give two alternatives for each one.

4 What makes a good set of instructions for getting to a place?

HOW DID YOU DO?

1 Which bit did you most enjoy? Can you explain what you liked about it?

2 In what ways is your work on this unit better than work you have done before?

3 If you had to go back to one section and do it again, which one would you choose and what would you do differently?

4 What would you like to improve about your story writing? What do you need to do to improve this skill?

5 What is the single most important thing you have to improve about your writing? How you might go about it?

UNIT TWO

The Village

In this unit you will imagine that you live or work in a village. You will take on the role of a villager and make up some information about your family, your job and your interests. You will find out about some important changes that are planned for your area. You will develop your skills as:

SPEAKERS AND LISTENERS

by talking about your ideas
by asking questions and making decisions
by learning different drama skills and acting out scenes

READERS

by reading information about your village
by reading a range of leaflets and articles

WRITERS

by writing notes and letters
by writing newspaper articles about your village

When you turn this page, you will see a map of a village…

Look carefully at this map of a village. In groups, discuss the following questions:

- Is it like anywhere you know?
- Where would people work in the village?
- Where would they do their shopping in the village?
- What is there for young people to do?
- Why would villagers sometimes have to go to a bigger town?
- Would there be any problems living in this village?
- What would you like about living here?

THE VILLAGE

IN THE NEWS

Even though the village is a fairly quiet place, there is always something going on. These headlines all come from the local newspaper.

Pupils Raise £200 in Charity Event

TROUBLE AT YOUTH CLUB

FEARS FOR MISSING PERSON

FIRST PRIZE FOR LOCAL WOMAN

POP STAR TO OPEN CHURCH FETE

CONCERN OVER CRIME RATE

Local Man in Rescue Drama

- Read through the headlines on page 37.

- In groups of four or five, discuss what you think each story could be about. For example, the first headline could be about some pupils at the village school who planned an event to raise money.

- Choose one of the stories which interests you. Act out a scene showing the story behind the headline. Refer to the Help Box below.

HELP

PLAY-MAKING

You have probably seen plays before. Perhaps you have seen a play performed in school or in a theatre. Follow the steps below to plan, prepare and perform a short scene in your group.

Step 1

Plan

Talk about and decide –
- who is involved
- where it takes place
- what happened

Step 2

Prepare

Talk about and decide –
- who plays each part
- what you have to say
- how it ends

Go through it a few times until you get it right.

Step 3

Perform

You don't need a stage or scenery but you may be able to use a few tables and chairs. Make sure –
- your audience is facing you
- you speak clearly
- you stay in your role

On your own, write up your news story. It might look something like this story.

Pupils Raise £200 in Charity Event

Pupils at Parkside School held a highly successful jumble sale for charity last week.

"I saw a programme on television about building new hospitals in Africa and I wanted to help," said Matthew Fisher, aged 11.

A group of pupils collected jumble and planned the event. Pupils and parents went along to the jumble sale and raised over £200.

Headteacher, Mrs Reid said, "The pupils did all the hard work. We just kept an eye on things and offered our help."

All the money raised will go straight to the charity 'Third World First'.

A spokesperson said, "We are delighted with the pupils' hard work. We will make sure that the money goes where it is needed."

There is talk of making this an annual event.

Make sure that you include –

* the names of people who are involved
* what they did
* a quote in speech marks

Your job is to tell the readers what happened as clearly as possible.

HELP

Newspaper Articles

The Headline:

The headline you have chosen gives you an outline of the whole story.

The beginning:

The first sentence can be a longer way of writing the headline. It gives more details about the headline.

The middle:

The middle sentences can report what somebody has said. Remember to use speech marks.

You can then include some more details about the story.

The end:

The last sentence could sum up the story. You could also say what might happen in the future.

WHO'S WHO?

Read through the information on these pages. Each role card
tells you about some of the people who live in the village.

The Bull Inn
Mr Spencer owns the local pub, The
Bull Inn. He employs a chef and some
bar staff to help him. The Bull Inn is
a very popular pub.

The Youth Club
The Youth Club is run by a youth
leader in the church hall and is open
every evening for young people aged
between 12 and 16. It is a good place
to learn new hobbies or just meet and
chat with your mates.

Brook Farm
Mr and Mrs Henderson live at Brook
Farm on the edge of the village.
There is a dairy on the farm where
Pat Fletcher works. There is also a
campsite on one of the fields.

R and J Motors
Ranjit Singh owns the local garage.
He employs a few other people as
mechanics and in the shop.

The Surgery
Dr Watson has worked in the village
for many years and knows most
people who live there. There is a
receptionist and a nurse who also
work at the Surgery.

Village Stores
Sarah Thompson runs the local shop
and post office. She sells newspapers,
groceries and videos. Her family help
in the shop when it is busy.

A DAY IN THE LIFE OF THE VILLAGE

- Get into a group of four or five. As a group, choose one of the role cards (on pages 40 and 41) that interests you. Each group in the class should choose a different one.

- Each role card tells you about one of the places in the village. It tells you about some of the people who live and work there. Decide who everyone in your group is going to be. Think about what they are doing. The role cards give you some ideas, but you will need to make up some different characters too. Talk about who you are to your group.

- You are going to make a **freeze frame** showing your characters. They might be serving a customer in the shop or pub, repairing a car in the garage or playing pool in the youth club. In your group, decide what you will all be doing and get into position for your freeze frame. Look at the Help Box below which tells you about freeze frames.

- Look at the freeze frame of another group. Talk about these questions together:

  Who do you think is in this freeze?

  What are they doing?

  Where do you think they are?

  How are these people feeling?

  What do you think they might be saying to one another?

- Now bring the freeze frame to life. Start off in your freeze frame and then bring it to life with movement and words for about one minute.

- What have you found out about the people in the village? Make a list of some of the things you have discovered about them. Who are they? What do they do? What are they like?

HELP

In a **freeze frame** the action is frozen, like when you press pause on a video.

You don't move or talk in a freeze frame. You have to get into a pose and keep still.

Think about –

- what you will be doing with your hands

- how you will be standing or sitting
- who and what you will be looking at
- the expression you will have on your face
- how you can use tables and chairs

Remember – don't move!
– don't talk!

MEET YOUR NEIGHBOUR

It would be a good idea to think a bit more about your characters.

- In your group, make up a few other details about who you are. Try to keep your ideas realistic. Talk about these questions.

  What is your name?
  How old are you?
  Where do you live?
  What is your job?
  Who else is in your family?
  What are your interests?

- Now write a role card for your character, like this:

Name:	Sam Henderson
Age:	17
Address:	Brook Farm
Job:	Study at the college in town. Help on the farm at weekends. Want to become a vet.
Family:	Live with mum and dad and younger brother, Tom.
Interests:	Go to Youth Club in village. Play guitar in a rock band.

- Get into pairs with someone from another group. You are both different people living and working in the village, but imagine you have never met.

- **Role-play** a short scene where you meet up for the first time. Look at the Help Box on page 44 if you need more information about role-play.

  You will need to decide where, when and how you meet. Try to find out as much as possible about one another. You will need to ask lots of questions and make up a few answers.

- When you are ready, show your scene to the class. Now you will find out about everyone else who lives in the village.

- Now choose one character from the village. It could be you or someone else. Write a more detailed description of the character. Try to include as much information as possible. It might start like this:

Hi, my name is Sam Henderson and I live with my mum and dad at Brook Farm. My hobbies are…

You could also draw a picture of what he or she looks like, or cut out a suitable photograph from a magazine.

HELP

ROLE-PLAY

When you are doing role-play, don't worry about making the scene look realistic. You don't need scenery or props. Just sit or stand facing your partner and talk. Try to talk and behave like the character you are playing. Think about what you say, rather than what you do.

HOT-SEATING

You could try hot-seating some of the characters. This is a bit like a television chat show or interview. The whole class sits in a circle and chooses one character. Everyone must keep asking them questions for about two minutes. The person being questioned must stay in role and talk as if he or she were really that character. You have to be good at making things up as you go along. This will help build up the character and make them seem more real.

BAD NEWS

One day, a letter comes through the door. It is addressed to
the head of the household. This is what is says.

Councillor Chris Hughes
Council Offices
Forest Road
Parkside
Leighton

27 September 1998

Dear Sir or Madam

You have already heard about the planned development in the village.
The Council is planning to carry out major building works to improve
facilities for everyone.

As your Councillor, I want to make sure that you have the chance to
find out more about the plans and make your views heard.

There will be a meeting in the Village Hall on Thursday at 7.30pm. I
hope you are able to attend.

Yours sincerely

C W Hughes

Councillor Chris Hughes

In your group, talk about these questions.

- Who is this letter from?
- Why is this person writing to everyone?
- What do you think these plans could be?

- How could they improve facilities in the village?
- When and where is the meeting?
- What will you say at the meeting?

THE MEETING

Everyone in the village wants to go along to the meeting to find out more about the plans. Meanwhile, you find some leaflets and articles which give you some more information. Study them carefully.

LEIGHTON POST

COUNCIL REVEALS PLANS FOR VILLAGE

The long-awaited plans for the village were revealed by the council yesterday. Land near the village centre is to be used for a much needed retail development. It will include a large supermarket, fast food outlet, a family pub, several smaller shops and parking for 200 cars.

Councillor Chris Hughes said he was delighted with the scheme. "The village badly needs new shops. I hope they will not only serve villagers' needs, but attract people from around the area as well."

Plans will go on display in the village hall next week and there will be a meeting next Thursday. The planning applications will be drawn up and sent to the Council's Planning Department towards the end of the year.

FOR SALE

20 acres of farmland near village centre. Suitable for residential or commercial development. To be sold by auction on May 12th.

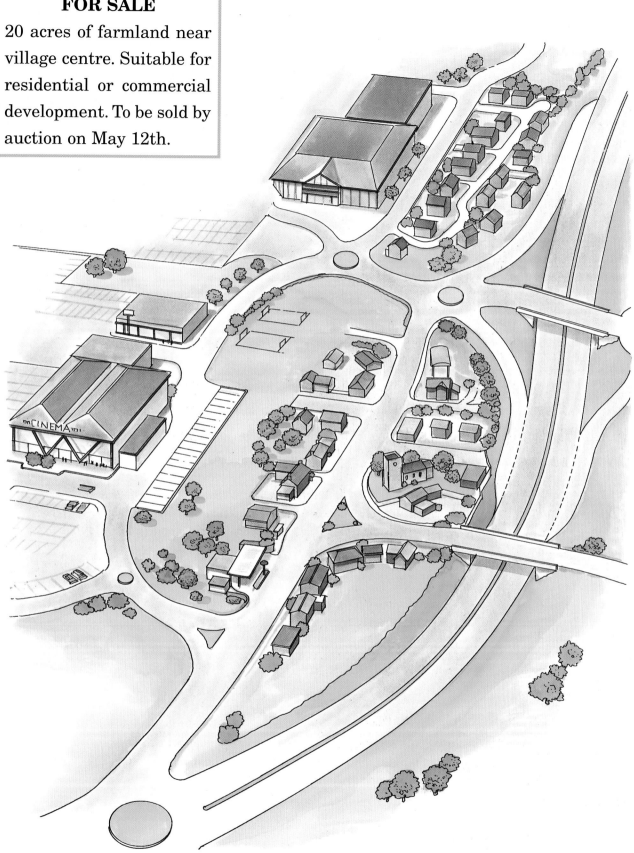

HELP

PLANNING THE MEETING

In real life people often go to meetings. Your teachers go to staff meetings to discuss what happens in school. In a meeting there is a chairperson. The chairperson makes sure only one person talks at once. Everyone has to keep to the point.

The whole class will take part in the meeting. You will play the character you have chosen to be. Your teacher will play the part of the chairperson, Councillor Hughes.

Put your chairs in a circle and remember that –

- you need to listen carefully to what everyone has to say

- you must not interrupt

- you have to stay in the role of your character

- After the meeting, discuss these questions:

Who was at the meeting?
What were the council's plans?
Who thought the plans would be a good idea?

Who did not think they were a good idea?
What did you think? Why?

- Copy the chart below and fill in the boxes showing what some of the different people thought of the plans. Say if they are for or against the plans and what their reasons are. Make sure you include yourself.

Name	What do they think of the plans?
Councillor Hughes	Councillor Hughes thinks that the new superstore will bring more business to the village. It will give villagers better shopping facilities.
Mr Spencer	
Ranjit Singh	

- What do you think would happen if the plans go ahead? Would it make more problems or make life better? How would the new development affect the people in your group? Plan, prepare and act out a scene showing what might happen if the new superstore is built.

A Letter to the Paper

After the meeting, you decide to write a letter to the local paper. You want to give your views on the plans. You will need to decide the layout of this letter. Follow the plan below to help you. Remember to use the name and address of your character from your drama.

HELP

WRITING THE LETTER

You should explain –

- what the plans are

- why you agree or disagree

- any other points made at the meeting

Try to sum up the reasons for or against the plans

	Your name Your address
	Date

Dear Editor,

I have been to a meeting about the Council's plans for the village. I have heard that they want to...
I think / don't think...
Some people at the meeting said...
Other people said...
In my opinion the Council should...

Yours faithfully,

Your signature

MAKE UP YOUR MIND

The Council decides to hold a second meeting before a decision is made.

Your teacher will be playing the role of the chairperson. You will be asked what you think about the plans. What will you say at the meeting?

HELP

PRESENTING YOUR VIEWS

- The meeting will start with the chairperson introducing everybody.

- Remember to listen to what other people have to say. They might make you change your mind.

- Make sure you get your views across. It will help if you have notes to remind you what to say.

- Don't be afraid to ask questions.

- At the end of the meeting, you will have to make a decision about the plans.

"If they build this shopping centre, there will be lots of traffic."

"It won't be long before there's an accident."

"You're right."

"I don't agree."

- Write a paragraph about what happened at the meeting.
- What was the decision?

WHAT NEXT?

The council listens to everyone's opinions and decides not to go ahead with the plans. This time the council decides to ask the people in the village first what they would like.

How do you think the village could be improved? Does it need anything else? Is there enough for young people? Perhaps money could be spent on some other improvements.

- In your group, discuss what you think the village most needs. Make a list of everyone's ideas. Choose one that you all agree on.

- Make a freeze frame (see page 42) showing your idea for an improvement. For example, you might show a freeze frame of children using new play equipment, people using a new pedestrian crossing or an event at a new community centre.

- Show your freeze frame to the class so that everyone can see it clearly. Then bring it to life with movement and words for about a minute.

- Hold a meeting for everyone in the village. Someone will need to chair the meeting. Each group will have the chance to put forward an idea. The meeting can discuss each one in turn and decide which one would be best for the village. Perhaps you could take a vote at the end of the meeting.

MEANWHILE, IN THE REAL WORLD ...

The people in the village decided to protest against plans to build a shopping centre, just as people sometimes do in real life. Perhaps you have heard about a similar campaign in the news, or maybe in your area.

One woman who became involved in a campaign was Jill Perry. A company called Nirex was planning to build a nuclear waste dump in Cumbria. Jill lived nearby and joined a protest group.

- Before reading Jill's story, talk about these questions.

Why do you think Jill was against these plans?

What do you think she did about it?

- Now read through Jill's story (below) to find out more. See if you can think of suitable words to fill in the gaps. Some words are suggested in the Help Box.

HELP

Word Bank

poor   children   teaching   important   father   population   dump   country   meet   council

"At the time I began to get involved I was teaching German," recalls Jill Perry, who is married and has two ___. "But I still felt I had some time on my hands. I thought I would like to do something and ___ some people. I had always been environmentally aware, but I had never been involved in anything."

"I was opposed to the idea because I had always felt uneasy about nuclear power. My ___ was a farmer and I remember in 1957, when there was a fire at Windscale, we had to ___ all the milk away. That certainly left an impression on me."

"It was not so much the science of it that bothered me at that stage – it was more the fact that Nirex had looked around the ___ for possible dump sites and of course had come up against

total opposition. It was obvious that the only place they felt they could build a ___ was somewhere that was nuclear-friendly, or dependent upon the industry. They assumed the local ___ would say, 'yes thanks, that's super!'"

Planning permission for the rock laboratory was turned down by Cumbria County ___. Almost immediately, Nirex appealed the decision. A public Inquiry was set for September 1995.

As the battle intensified, Jill made the decision to resign from ___ and devote herself full-time to the campaign.

"I liked the school where I was teaching, and I really enjoyed my job. Resigning did not help my career, but I knew it was ___ to work on the campaign."

(from 'Earthmatters' published by Friends of the Earth)

A public enquiry was held and lasted for nearly two years.
After the enquiry the Government refused to give Nirex
planning permission to build the dump.

- Imagine that Jill is being interviewed on a TV chat show. Here are some questions that the interviewer could ask her.

  When did you first become concerned about nuclear power?

  Why did you set up a Friends of the Earth group?

  Why were you against the nuclear waste dump?

  What did your family think about what you were doing?

  How did you protest against the nuclear waste dump?

  How did you feel when the plans were turned down?

- Can you think of any other questions to ask her? You could make up questions about her family, her job and her opinions, as well as her involvement in the campaign against nuclear waste. Write down your questions.

- Your teacher or another adult can play the role of Jill in the TV interview. The whole class can ask her questions. Listen carefully to what she says and make notes on her answers.

- When you have finished asking questions, write out your interview. It might look like this:

  Interviewer: *When did you first become concerned about nuclear power?*
  Jill: *My dad was a farmer and I remember in 1957 there was a fire at the nuclear power station. My dad had to throw away all the milk because it could have become radioactive. I realised that nuclear power was very unsafe.*

  This form of writing is called **script**.

Script is another way of writing speech. It is a way of showing what the characters of a play say or what people say to each other in films or on TV.

WHAT DID YOU LEARN?

You have read leaflets, written articles and used drama to learn about your village. Now answer the questions below:

1 What have you learned about drama from this unit?
   Can you explain:

   Role Play

   Freeze Frame

   Character

   Hot Seating

2 What part did you play in the two meetings? What did you have to say? How well did others in your class do?

HOW DID YOU DO?

1 Which part of this unit did you most enjoy? Can you explain what you liked about it?

2 In what ways is this work better than work you have done before?

3 What, if anything, did you find difficult in this unit?

4 What would you like to improve about your drama work? What do you need to do to improve your drama skills?

UNIT THREE

Poetry Alive

In this unit you have the chance to read a lot of different poems. You will also improve your skills as:

SPEAKERS AND LISTENERS

by listening to poems
by reading aloud

READERS

by reading different types of poem
by learning about how poems work

WRITERS

by writing your own poems
by writing down your thoughts about the poems

In this unit, keep all your work in your own poetry book. Your poetry book can be used to:
- write down any unusual words
- note down any feelings you have about a poem
- jot down the lines of poetry you like best...

WHAT IS A POEM?

You are going to think about the difference between a poem
and a piece of ordinary prose writing.
Look at these two pieces of writing.

1 Prose

This passage comes from an
encyclopaedia.

Centipede:

the name means 'hundred-legged'.
Centipedes have bodies that are made
of many segments. Each segment has
a pair of legs. Fully grown centipedes
may have as many as 177 pairs of legs.

The common centipede has only thirty
legs. It lives in damp places and feeds
at night on insects. It is harmless.

The female covers her eggs with a
sticky liquid and rolls them in earth to
keep the male from eating them.

Centipedes move quickly and kill their
prey with poison fangs. There is one
kind of centipede which is 28 cms long
and can kill small birds.

2 Poetry

This is a poem.

A CENTIPEDE

A centipede can run at great speed
Because of his number of legs,
But when he hangs out his socks to dry,
It costs him a fortune in pegs.

A centipede likes to wear wellington boots,
But because of his centipede brain,
It takes such a time to sort out all the pairs
That he's never in time for the rain.

A centipede has one hundred legs,
But I'm glad that I haven't because
When the front of the centipede gets
where it's going
His back end is still where it was.

Julie Hodder

- Make a list of the differences you can see between prose and poetry.

Think about the way they look on the page.

Think about the way they sound.

Think about the way they are expressed.

Set your work out like this:

Prose	*Poetry*

- Now it is your turn to be a poet!

   Either: Write another verse for the centipede poem, using the same **rhyme**, **rhythm** and **structure**. You can choose one of these first lines:

A centipede likes to wear ballet shoes

or

A centipede likes to play Twister

or

A centipede loves to go dancing

Or: Write your own centipede poem, choosing your own rhyme, rhythm and structure. Here are some ideas to help you.

A poem in the shape of a centipede

or

A poem about the vicious side of the centipede

or

A poem expressing the centipede's thoughts.

HELP

Rhyme = words that sound the same.

Rhythm = the beat made by the words in a poem.

Structure = the way a poem is put together.

ALLITERATION

Read this rather odd poem.

> Creepy Carla creates cool crocodile cocktails
> Jolly John jumps over jellies
> Lovely Laura loves licking lollipops
> Humorous Helen hugs humungous hippos
> Ridiculous Rachel runs races in the rain
> Terrible Tom tickled ten talented Turkish tigers

- With a partner, choose one line to read again.
- What do you notice about the first sound of each word?
- Where have you seen this before? Does 'Pick up a Penguin' give you a clue? Repeating a letter at the beginning of each word is called **alliteration**.

A class of your age made this poem up.
Each member of the class described
themselves using words that began
with the first letter of their first name.

Your class could write a poem the same way.

Or you could write an alphabet song or book for young readers to learn.

Or you could write a slogan or advert for a TV commercial.

You can use your dictionary or thesaurus to help.

ONOMATOPOEIA

When you use words which sound like the noise they make,
this is known as **onomatopoeia**.

Make a class list of **onomatopoeic** words.
Here are some words to start your list:

pop	bang	guffaw
crack	crash	roar
smash	hum	splat

Poets often use onomatopoeia when writing poems. Sounds are very important. They make the poem 'alive'.

Now read this poem.

PING-PONG

Swatted between bats
The celluloid ball
Leaps on unseen elastic
Skimming the taut net.

Sliced	Spun
Screwed	Cut
Dabbed	Smashed

    Point
      Service

Ping	Pong
Pong	Ping
Bing	Bong
Bong	Bing

    Point
      Service

Ding	Dong
Dong	Ding
Ting	Tong
Tang	Tong

    Point
   Service

Angled	Slipped
Bit	Bat
Tip	Tap
Slip	Slap
Zip	Zap
Whip	Whap

    Point
      Service

Left	Yes
Right	Yes
Twist	Yes
Skids	Yes
Eighteen	Seventeen
Eighteen	All
Nineteen	Eighteen
Nineteen	All
Twenty	Nineteen

    Point
      Service

Forehand	Backhand
Swerves	Yes
Rockets	Yes
Battered	Ah
Cut	Driven
Floated	Caressed
Driven	Hammered

    THWACKED
Point
Service

Cracked	Ah

    SMASHED
     SMASHED
      SMASHED
    GAME

Gareth Owen

- Listen to the **sounds** in the poem – you can **hear** the ball being hit.

- Divide the class into two teams and one narrator.

	= narrator
	= blue team
	= green team
	= whole class

- Try reading the poem using the colour to warn you when it's your team's turn to read together. Practise until you get the timing right. You can see how the poem really captures the sounds, pace and excitement of the ping-pong match.

Now you are going to write your own **onomatopoeic** poem.

1. Choose one of these ideas for a poem (or use an idea of your own).

at the dentist's   at a disco

at a football match   two dogs fighting

a parade   in a kitchen making a meal

at a concert   at a fireworks display

at the swimming pool   at any sporting competition

2. Next, make a list of sounds, words and actions. For example:

At a football match:		
kick	*whack*	*slam*
tackle	*run*	*race*
chase	*dodge*	*swerve*
shoot	*heading*	*dribble*
cheering	*penalty*	*corner*
kick-off	*referee*	*the whistle shrills*
the crowd roars	*come on the Reds*	*the teams are ready*
Go Blues Go	*one-nil*	*GOAL!*

3. Now use some of your words to write the first verse of the poem so it sets the scene in three lines. For example:

> The teams are ready
>
> The crowds are waiting
>
> The whistle shrills

4. Next, write a few lines of paired words like this:

> Go Reds Go   Go Blues Go
>
> run   dodge
>
> swerve   tackle
>
> kick   slam

5. Then bring it to a sudden climax like this:

> GOAL!

6. Repeat this pattern two or three more times to give you a complete poem in the style of 'Ping-Pong'.

RHYME

Rhymes are made when two words sound the same. For example:

leg – peg

spoon – moon

In this poem, words that sound the same are placed at the end of the lines. The rhymes in this poem have been left out. Can you work out what they are?

ROGER THE DOG

Asleep he wheezes at his ease.
He only wakes to scratch his   A   .

He hogs the fire, he bakes his head
As if it were a loaf of   B   .

He's just a sack of snoring dog.
You can lug him like a   C   .

You can roll him with your foot,
He'll stay snoring where he's   D   .

I take him out for exercise.
He rolls in cowclap up to his   E   .

He will not race, he will not romp,
He saves his strength for gobble and   F   .

He'll work as hard as you could wish
Emptying his dinner   G   .

Then flops flat, and digs down deep,
Like a miner, into   H   .

Ted Hughes

- Compare your guesses with a partner. Choose the best suggestion.
  You can find the words used by the poet on page 76.
- The pairs of rhyming lines are known as **rhyming couplets**. Why 'couplets'?

- What other clues did you use besides rhyme to help you?
- Can you find examples in the poem of:
  onomatopoeia
  alliteration?

RHYTHM

Now read this poem.

THE MONSTER

The mighty monster marched
Through silty, slimy swamp.
Fourteen feet a footstep,
With a clattering, crashing clomp.
His eerie but excellent eyes,
His terrible tyrannous teeth,
Dribbled and dripped as he dashed
To the beautiful banquet beneath.
Maids and men were merrily munching
Bread, beef and beer of the best,
Unaware of the ugly, unwelcome,
Gate-crashing, gigantic guest.
Shouts and shrieks of shock,
Bellowing and beating of breasts,
As the monster munched the menu,
And greedily gobbled the guests.

This is a brilliant poem to act out!
It has got a very strong beat.
When you act it out you will hear it.

- Split into five groups: A, B, C, D, E.
- *Group A*:

Keep the beat of the poem. You are the sound of the monster marching. This is **a very important job**!
You can do this by marching or by clapping your hands or tapping the desk.

- *Other groups*:

Watch out for your lines, then read them aloud when it is your turn.

Group B	The mighty monster marched
	Through silty, slimy swamp.
	Fourteen feet a footstep,
	With a clattering, crashing clomp.
Group C	His eerie but excellent eyes,
Group D	His terrible tyrannous teeth,
Group E	Dribbled and dripped as he dashed
	To the beautiful banquet beneath.
Group B	Maids and men were merrily munching
Group C	Bread, beef and beer of the best,
Group D	Unaware of the ugly, unwelcome,
	Gate-crashing, gigantic guest.
Group E	Shouts and shrieks of shock,
Group B	Bellowing and beating of breasts,
Group C	As the monster munched the menu,
ALL	**And greedily gobbled the guests.**

COLOUR POEMS

The following poems are about the feelings we have when we think of a colour. For example:

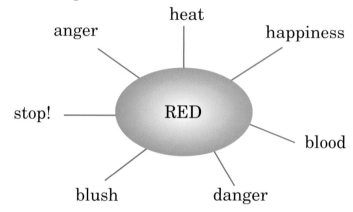

Make spider diagrams in your poetry book for these colours in the same way:

GREEN   BLACK   YELLOW   WHITE

Now read these two colour poems.

ORANGE

An inviting fire glowing brightly
A flickering candle flame
A comforting warmth
Or a good feeling
The forthcoming heat
On a fresh summer morning.

Charlotte Bourne

TURQUOISE

A calm sea floating on nothing,

Tumbling waterfalls from a deep rock face,

A glowing jewel giving off a special light,

Never-ending holes that fall for miles and miles,

Dolphins leaping in the air,

Quiet, peaceful, understanding, flowing.

Emma Louise Phillips

You are now going to write your own colour poem.

- Choose one of your colour spider diagrams.

- Write your colour as the title for your poem in your poetry book.

- There is one rule. You cannot use the name of the colour in your poem. Instead you must describe it.

- Draft your first attempt.

- Read it to a partner. Are you pleased? If not, make some changes.

- When you are happy with your work, write it out neatly.

- Add illustrations to your finished work.

The following poems are full of colour.

Each colour helps to make a different picture in your mind.

JAMAICA MARKET

Honey, pepper, leaf-green limes,

Pagan fruit whose names are rhymes

Mangoes, breadfruit, ginger-roots,

Granadillas, bamboo-shoots,

Cho-cho, ackees, tangerines,

Lemons, purple Congo-beans,

Sugar, okras, kola-nuts,

Citrons, hairy coconuts,

Fish, tobacco, native hats,

Gold bananas, woven mats,

Plantains, wild-thyme, pallidleeks,

Pigeons with their scarlet beaks,

Oranges and saffron yams,

Baskets, ruby guava jams,

Turtles, goat-skins, cinnamon,

Allspice, conch-shells, golden rum.

Black skins, babel – and the sun

That burns all colours into one.

Agnes Maxwell-Hall

- On a copy of the poem, colour over the words which name a colour. Use the right colour.

- Colour over the names of objects which have a special colour. For example, banana = yellow.

- This poem uses our senses to bring the Jamaican market to life. Which senses does it use?

- For each sense, find an example of a word in the poem which awakens that sense.

- What impression has the poet given you of a Jamaican market?

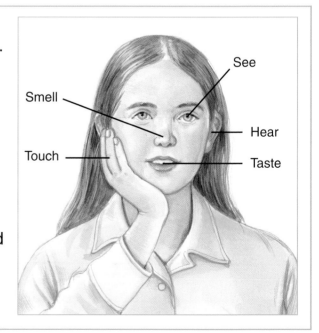

PROSE POEM

The days are gold,
and the evenings filled with golden light
as the sun sets.
It is paddy-threshing time,
the great stacks near their heads
little brittle brown-haired men
but the egrets sprinkle a snow-storm.
How beautiful their line of flight,
the positioning of their legs,
and their wings – so soft white
against the golden sun.
It is winter now – but a winter running away.
The wheat is growing: a sturdy deep-set green
the days are all green and gold
and the birds bring the extra colour –
the jay its blue, the barbets lemon
amidst the green
leaves, which rustle, sing, wave hands,
count fingers,
pollenfilled blossoms drift –
and a drift of poems in the breeze.

Monika Varma

GLOSSARY

paddy-threshing = beating grain to separate it from its husk

brittle = easily broken

egret = a white bird, rather like a heron

barbet = a yellow bird

- On a copy of this poem, shade over the words which suggest colours to you. Some words name the colour and some words just hint at it.

- Why has the poet used these colours?

- In your poetry book, illustrate the poem. Draw the pictures that the poem brings into your mind.

SIMILE

- Here are some well-known **similes**:

as cold as ice   as flat as a pancake

as cunning as a fox   as light as a feather

as quick as lightning   as slow as a snail

Do you know more similes? Make a list!

- Read the poem 'Flashlight' below. How is a flashlight like a hound? Find as many points of comparison as you can.

> A **simile** is a way of describing something by comparing it with something else. You will learn more about similes in the next unit

FLASHLIGHT

My flashlight tugs me
through the dark
like a hound
with a yellow eye,

        sniffs
        at the edges
        of steep places,

paws
at moles'
and rabbits'
holes,

        points its nose
        where sharp things
        lie asleep –

and then it bounds
ahead of me
on home ground.

Judith Thurman

THE SEA

Today the sea is playful and
casts a white froth across the sand
like the flounces on a long blue gown
which is shifting gently up and down.

Who would think it would rage
like a great giant in a cage
swallowing sailor, ship and boat
and sucking them swiftly down its throat?

Iain Crichton Smith

- Find the word *like* in the first verse. What is the sea like? Explain the comparison.

- Find the word *like* in the second verse. What is the sea like here?

- Draw the sea. Make it look like the way it is described in either the first or second verse.

In the poem on the next page, fog is described as a creature.

FOG

Over the oily swell it heaved, it rolled,
Like some foul creature, filmy, nebulous.
It pushed out streaming tentacles, took clammy hold,
Swaddled the spars, wrapped us in damp and cold,
Blotted the sun, crept round and over us.
Day long, night long, it hid us from the sky –
Hid us from sun and stars as in a tomb.
Shrouded in mist a berg went groaning by.
Far and forlorn we heard the blind ships cry.
Like lost souls wailing in a hopeless gloom.
Like a bell-wether clanging from the fold,
A codder called her dories. With scared breath
The steamer syrens shrieked; and mad bells tolled.
Through time eternal in the dark we rolled
Playing a game of Blind-Man's Buff with Death.

Crosbie Garstin (1887–1930)

GLOSSARY

nebulous = hazy, like a cloud

swaddled = wrapped or bandaged

spars = masts of a ship

shrouded = wrapped in coffin clothes

berg = ice berg

forlorn = sad

bell-wether = a bell hanging round the neck of leading male sheep

codder = ship carrying fish (cod)

dories = small flat-bottomed boats

syrens = signal or warning sound

• Read the first verse again. Look at the words used to describe the creature:

Foul = dirty, nasty

Filmy = misty

Nebulous = cloudy

These are all **adjectives**. Adjectives are words which describe objects. Can you find anymore?

• Now make a list of all the words used to describe the movements of the fog. For example: Heaved

These are **verbs** or doing words. Find as many as you can.

• Write down the words that make you think the fog is a creature.

• Now draw this creature.
What colours would it be?
Why have you decided to use these colours?
What do the 'streaming tentacles' look like?
Why do you think that the tentacles look like this?

METAPHOR

Now read this poem, which uses metaphors to describe the members of a family.

> A **metaphor** is when an object is described as something else without using the words 'like' or 'as'.

THE ANIMAL HOUSE

I have a lion, a furry faced lion.
He dominantly controls the household.
He eats a lot of meat and he snarls if I pester him.
He is out most of the day. I call him Dad.

I also have a dove.
She works all day too, but she works at home.
She is soft, gentle, kind and cares for her young.
She is always there if I need her. I call her Mum.

I have a peacock.
She has a head with lots of different colours.
She has green eyes and a beautiful coat.
She has a tuff of glittery hair at the front. I call her my punk sister.

I have a kitten.
He is so small and smooth.
He has teeny little eyes and a wet nose.
He drinks milk a lot, and cries a lot. I call him baby brother.

Then there's me.
I know what I am.
I'm the black sheep.

Sandy Brechin

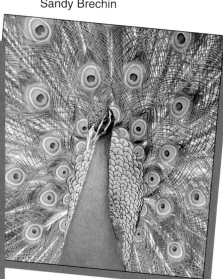

- Choose three people to write a poem about.
  They could be friends, members of your family or even famous people you would like to meet.

- To get started you will need to make notes on each person.
  You can use these questions to help you prepare your poem.

  What is the name of the person?

  Which animal do they remind you of?

  In what ways does the person's character, movement, sounds or looks match the animal you have chosen?

  Make notes using a grid like this:

Name	
Animal	
Sound	
Movement	
Character	
Looks	

- With a partner, study 'The Animal House' and discuss these questions:
  What do you notice about the start of each verse?
  How does the last line of each verse end?
  How many lines are there for each verse?
  This is the pattern:
  Line 1:   I have a ...
  Line 2:   He/she...
  Line 3:   He/she...
  Line 4:   He/she...   I call him/her...

- Now use your notes to write one verse for each person. You can use the pattern of 'The Animal House' to write your poem.

- Finally, how do the animal metaphors in 'The Animal House' make you feel about the people they describe? Do you think the poem is a good description of a family?

WHAT DID YOU LEARN?

In this unit you have looked at what makes poetry come alive.
Ask yourself the following questions:

1 What are the differences between poetry and prose?
2 What is alliteration? Give three examples from the poetry
   you have read.
3 What is onomatopoeia? Give three examples from the poetry
   you have read.
4 What jobs do rhyme and rhythm do in a poem?
5 What other things bring poetry to life?

WRITING ABOUT A POEM

As an extension to the work you have done, you may like to write
about a poem of your choice.

• Ask your teacher for books with poems in them.
  We call a collection of poems an **anthology**.

• Look for interesting poems and read them aloud to your group.

• Choose one poem you like best of all and write about it like this:
  My favourite poem is called..., and is written by...
  It is about...
  The thing I like about it is...
  Some striking words are used. For example...
  There are also some unusual ideas such as...
  The poem appeals to the sense of sight by...
  For example...
  It also appeals to other senses such as...
  For example...
  Its rhythm is... so that...
  The poem makes me think of...
  When I first read it I felt... especially when...
  What the poet really wants to say is...
  I think...

Use extra sentences if you need them.

sleep	chomp	put	bread
dish	eyes	log	fleas

UNIT FOUR

Language Investigators

In this unit, you will become a language investigator. You will study how language works and develop your skills as:

SPEAKERS AND LISTENERS

by finding ways to communicate clearly
by working as a team on games and activities

READERS

by studying the way words and sentences are put together
by solving language puzzles

WRITERS

by studying spelling, punctuation and grammar
by improving written work

In this unit, you will be contacted by strange beings. They will ask you questions about your language. Turn the page to meet...

...COMMANDER XELPOP

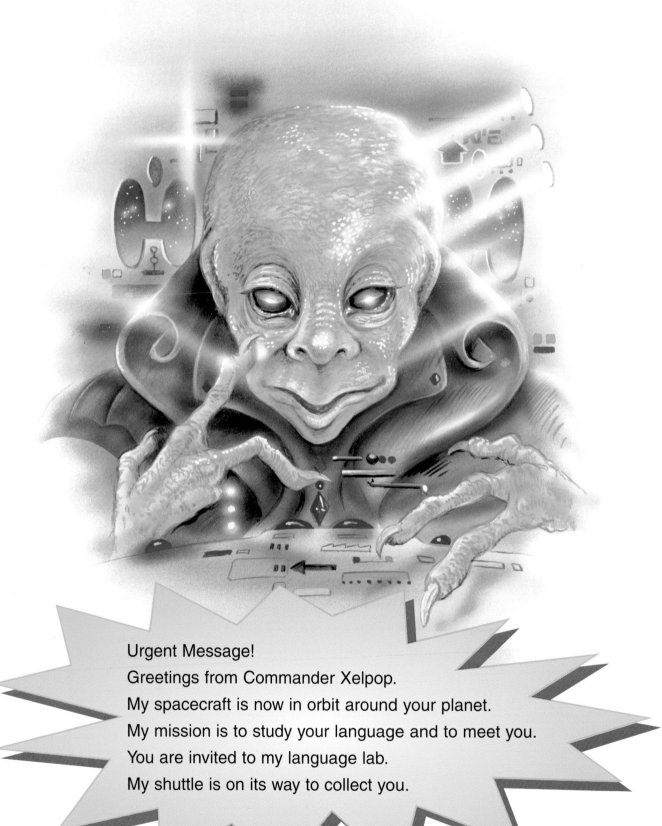

Urgent Message!

Greetings from Commander Xelpop.

My spacecraft is now in orbit around your planet.

My mission is to study your language and to meet you.

You are invited to my language lab.

My shuttle is on its way to collect you.

Sounds like a job for…

…THE LANGUAGE INVESTIGATORS!

Your task is to enter the alien language lab and make contact.

Tell them everything they need to know.

WELCOME TO THE LANGUAGE LAB

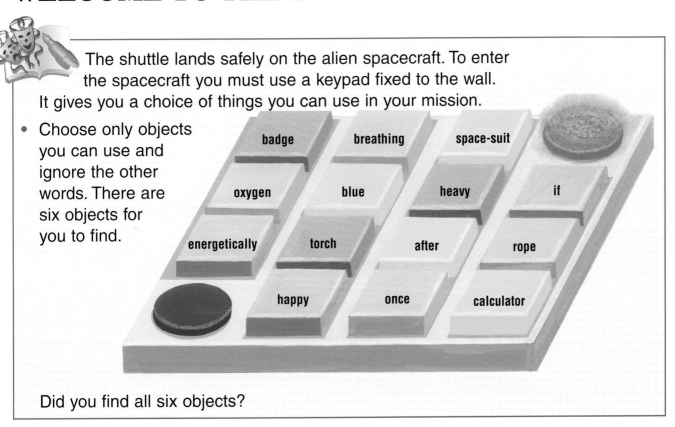

The shuttle lands safely on the alien spacecraft. To enter the spacecraft you must use a keypad fixed to the wall. It gives you a choice of things you can use in your mission.

• Choose only objects you can use and ignore the other words. There are six objects for you to find.

badge   breathing   space-suit

oxygen   blue   heavy   if

energetically   torch   after   rope

happy   once   calculator

Did you find all six objects?

Ordinary words which name things are called **nouns.**

A noun is a label given to a person, thing, feeling or idea.

If you can use the word 'the' before the word, it's probably a noun.

SCANNED!

When you enter the spacecraft, you are scanned by the ship's computer. The computer lists a number of things it knows about you. They are all nouns.

There are four kinds of noun:

Common noun – an ordinary thing (e.g. table, chair, pen)

Proper noun – a name or title (e.g. Simon, Queen Mary, Bell Road). A proper noun always has a capital letter.

Abstract noun – a feeling, a quality or an idea (e.g. joy, love, fear, interest)

Collective noun – a group of things or people (e.g. gang, herd, team, flock)

intelligence
helmet
Earth
tubes
Commander
team
J. Munroe
gloves
curiosity
pimple
Space-camp
surprise
family
fear
space-suit
badge

• Take the words from the scan above and write them in the correct box on a grid like this. The first two have been done to start you off.

Common	Proper	Abstract	Collective
helmet		*intelligence*	

• Add three extra words of your own in each box.
• Now design your own alien using the four different kinds of nouns to label it.
• Draw another table and list your words about the alien in the same way.

THE CHALLENGE

You are now challenged to a game of noun volleyball by the computer.

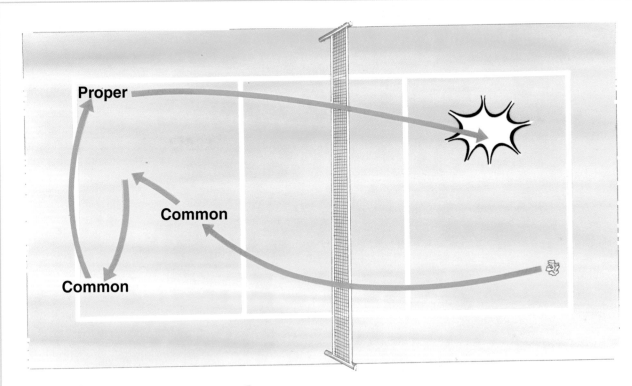

To play this game you need:

a) Two teams: one for the computer, one for the Language Investigators.

b) A screwed-up piece of paper.

Rules:

1 You *serve* to the other team by calling out an **abstract** noun.

2 You *keep* the ball in the air by calling out a **common** noun.

3 You *return* the ball back to the other team by calling out a **proper** noun.

4 Only the person holding the ball can call out a noun.

5 A noun can only ever be used once.

6 You must pass the ball within five seconds.

Aim of the game:

To get the opposing team to make as many mistakes as possible!

Train for the game:

Prepare a list of abstract, common and proper nouns to help you play the game.

THE FIX

The door into the next room on the spacecraft will not open. You must cut the correct wire in the control box to open the door. Choose the wrong wire and you will be unable to go any further.

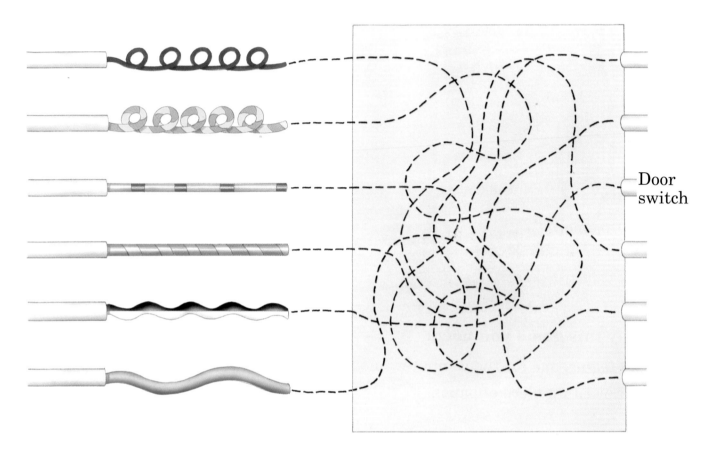

Door switch

What colour is the correct wire?

• Your colour eye-sights have failed. You can see only in black and white.
How can you describe each wire without using colour?

Use the sentences below to help you.

Don't cut the _____ and _____ wire.
Don't cut the _____ and _____ wire.
Don't cut the _____ and _____ wire.
Don't cut the _____ and _____ wire.
Don't cut the _____ and _____ wire.
Do cut the _____ and _____ wire.

The words you have used to describe the wires are called **adjectives.**

Every adjective describes a noun. In this case, the noun is the wire.

On a display in the room behind the door are plants and
animals collected during trips around the galaxy.

- For each exhibit, write down four adjectives to describe it.
- Make up four more exhibits of your own, and include four
adjectives in the same way.

ACTION!

A friendly robot asks you if you'd like a cup of coffee.
It comes to you cold and most of it is in your lap,
not in the cup.

There must be something wrong with the robot's
programme for making coffee!
Looking at the programme you find this:

Coffee-making programme:

1 WASH KETTLE WITH WATER

2 INVITE PLUG INTO ENERGY
   SOCKET

3 ROAST WATER

4 SHOVEL COFFEE INTO CUP

5 THROW WATER INTO CUP

6 SIEVE THE MIXTURE

7 SHIFT THE CUP

- What is wrong? Can you explain why you get a cold lump of coffee in your lap rather than a hot cup of coffee to drink?

- Pick out the words which cause the problem in each sentence.
These words are called **verbs.**
Verbs are action words e.g. jump, talk, grow.

- Replace the problem verbs with new ones to make the programme run more smoothly and give you a hot cup of coffee.

The robot can now make a decent cup of coffee but it moves rather oddly. It only knows a few actions as it has only been programmed with just a few verbs. It can:

wash	walk	roast	look	shovel	start
invite	hold	throw	stop	sieve	shift

- What other verbs will the robot need to know before it can clean the cabin?
  Write a programme and underline the new verbs. Start like this:

  PROGRAMME: Clean the cabin
  1 <u>Sweep</u> the floor
  2 <u>Dust</u> … now you continue

- Now make a list of new verbs the robot will need to complete the task list below:

Task list:

1 Peel an orange

2 Guard the space shuttle

3 Load the cargo bay with supplies

4 Play volleyball with the earthlings

- Write one more programme and test it on a friend. Your friend can play the part of the robot, to see if the programme makes sense.

CONTACT!

Before you can enter the next room in the spacecraft you must reconnect the word circuit to make four sentences.

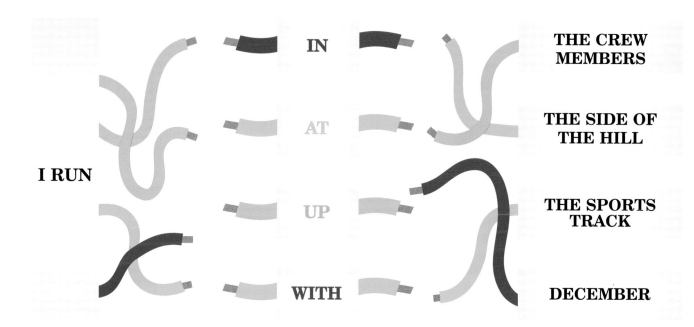

The middle group of words help to show one of four things:
the place
the position
the time
the way of doing.

These important words are called **prepositions.**

Other prepositions are:

into	around	up	over	through	between	out
along	underneath	down	under	in	across

Suddenly you find yourself in a dark room. You have to make your way using a map.

- Study the map of the room below. Make a list of the prepositions you need. Then write the instructions for getting through.

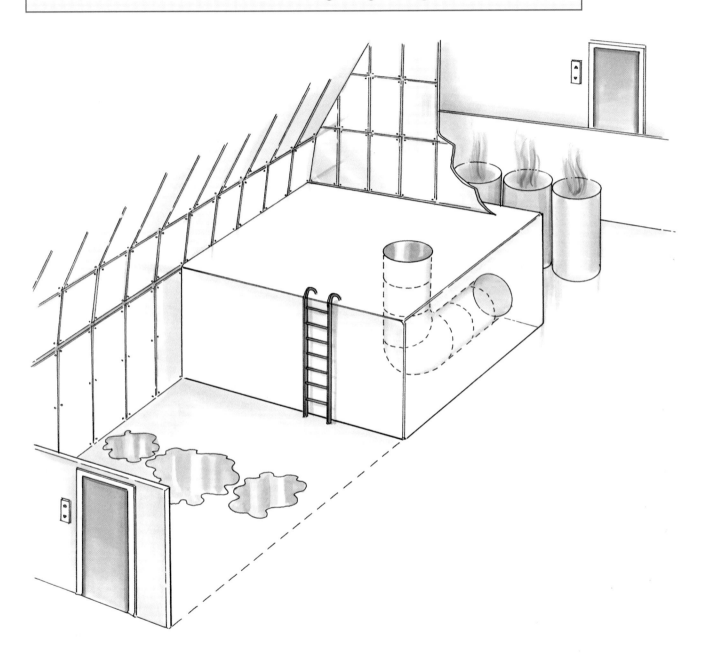

HOW DO YOU COMMUNICATE?

As you leave the last room, the door opens to the Control Room. You see before you the alien race who have travelled far to see Earth. No-one speaks.

You decide to mime your greetings.

You need to:

1 Greet them

2 Show them you come in peace

3 Make it clear who you are

4 Make them understand the dangers of space, before they send you out again

5 Try to teach them some important nouns

- In pairs, work out your mimes.
- Show your mimes to another pair. Watch their mimes.
- Did you understand each other's mimes?

After enjoying your mimes, the aliens decide to talk.

Well, thanks. Impressive stuff. Acting like we also. But on to the stuff serious shall we go? Look, we'd know more to like about your language. List we have of dictionaries in your words but clear we are not order about the. Matter it does? Under me do you stand. Can you? Help!

- • What answer will you give?
  - • Does it matter if words are in the wrong order?
- • What are the rules about the order of words in a sentence?
  Try to explain to the aliens how a basic sentence works, using the following information:

  The **subject** is the person or thing in the sentence that does something.

  The object is the person or thing in the sentence that something happens to.

  For example: **Peter** hit James

Remember that you have already met:

  nouns
  verbs
  prepositions
  adjectives

- • Can you tell Commander Xelpop anything about the order of words in a simple sentence?
  Use these sentences to show what you mean:

  We welcome you to Earth.
  We come in peace to see you.
  Your robot makes a good cup of coffee.
  Earthlings don't eat sewage.
  We have had a big breakfast already.
  Thank you, we'll eat later.

LAST SEEN WEARING A SPACECRAFT

Now show the aliens how to organise their sentences by sorting out their last report to the home planet.

> This is a quick report about our contact with the earthlings Language Lab the latest in.
> I up woke to the rest of the crew find worried excited and. Claim to have they a creature large, wearing a spacecraft outside of the floating space-suit. It was went by as it waving to them! By the time fifteen all of us had our way tripped and clambered there was nothing there to the landing dock. Left was the space-suit the only thing, still swinging on its owner where the hook left it had. When back to rest our room got we, the spacecraft felt we all shake.
> Engines had started the someone.

- Write the report putting the words in the correct order.
  - Underline all the adjectives.
- Where do adjectives usually go?
- Circle all the verbs.
- Where do the verbs usually go?
- Which usually comes first – the subject or the object?

FLIP-BOOK FOR THE ALIENS

Using your knowledge of sentences, create a short book for young aliens, telling them about your space journey, and helping them to learn your language in a fun way. Follow the steps below:

HOW TO MAKE A FLIP-BOOK

Step 1

Think of four short sentences. Divide the sentences into four headings. Set your work out like this:

subject	verb	preposition	object
The captain	*said no*	*to*	*another helping of slime pie*
I	*flew*	*in*	*the spacecraft*

Step 2

Look at the diagram above. Make each line into one page of the flip-book. Cut around each word so it can be turned over on its own.

Step 3

Have fun seeing what combinations of sentences you can make.

Step 4

You can also increase your library of flip-books with other stories about Earth:

    the farm

    the zoo

    the town.

You may want to add adjectives and adverbs to your flip-book.

GIFTS

The aliens have presented you with some gifts.

The robot below is loading them onto the space shuttle.

The robot has six minutes to load the gifts before the loading bay doors open and everything is blown out into space!

It takes one minute to complete each line in its computer programme.

If you could join the lines together it would save precious time.

- Find a way of joining the commands together to make just six lines.

Programme for loading bay robot:
Robot finds the correct container.
Robot grasps container in its lifting claw.
Robot turns around to face the loading bay.
Robot locates the correct space shuttle.
Robot moves slowly down the main corridor.
Robot watches carefully for any Investigators in the way.
Robot realises Investigators will not get out of the way.
Robot lets Investigators pass.
Robot moves quickly down an empty corridor.
Robot approaches the loading door of the correct shuttle.
Robot presses the button to release the loading door.
Robot proceeds up the ramp.
Robot releases the container in the shuttle.

- Once you have loaded the cargo successfully, write your own programme for an everyday task that has at least ten commands, but only five sentences.
  For example:
    making a phone call
    making coffee
    having a bath.

HELP

Connectives

Connectives link two sentences.

I went into the space shuttle. I flew to the spacecraft.

If you add the most common connective

and

this happens:

I went into the space ~~_____~~ *and flew to the spacecraft.*

Most people use **and**. However, there are many more connectives to make ideas join in exciting ways.

Here are just a few:

but	therefore	before
because	while	so
however	after	when

Try writing one long sentence containing all these connectives.

A SMALL MISUNDERSTANDING

Commander Xelpop speaks. Read aloud his speech, including the sound effects he uses.

Welcome (cough) earthlings (sneeze) It (sniff) s a pleasure to welcome you aboard (sneeze) We (sniff) ve been looking forward to your visit (sneeze) Have the crew made you comfortable (choke) I hope they gave you slime pies (sneeze) I said to Pipop the cook (cough tut-tut) Make slime pies (sneeze) No one can resist them (blow tut-tut) Now let me introduce you to my staff (yawn) Gog (cough) Drex (cough) Flup and Goor (sneeze) Anyone care for a drink of rat (sniff) s blood (choke)

- What are the strange sound effects?
- On a grid like this, work out the meaning of each sound effect:

Sound	Meaning
sneeze	
cough	
tut tut	
sniff	
choke	
blow	
yawn	

Punctuation marks... What are they for? Why do you not sound them out when you speak?

I think I can explain about the strange sound effects – they're punctuation marks.

- Commander Xelpop has asked two very good questions. Can you answer them? Use a grid like this:

Mark	Name	What it is for
.	*Full stop*	*1 To end a sentence* *2 Warning that a new sentence may well start here.*
،	*Comma*	
،	Apostrophe	
!	Exclamation mark	
?		
" "		
;		

HELP

Tell me, what is the sign of the tadpole for?

Commander Xelpop is talking about commas!

The answer to his question is:

1 To break up long sentences so the reader can see how it works.

2 To show when you move the end bit of a sentence to the front or middle of it. For example:

Have some Gallian snake guts **before you go.**

Before you go, do have some Gallian snake guts.

Find a reading book and find 10 examples of sentences which use commas in this way.

Just then, a group of word workers arrive to take you on a
tour of the word labs. They take you through a door:

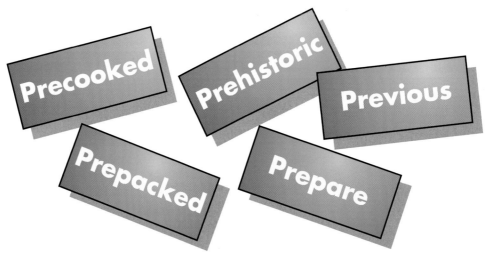

The word sorting office

In the sorting room, the aliens are busy grouping words. One
of the piles contains these words:

Precooked **Prehistoric** **Previous**

Prepacked **Prepare**

• Can you explain to the aliens what **pre** means in these words?

There are other piles:

Recycle
Repeat
Return
Repay
Remember

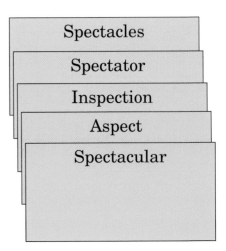

Spectacles
Spectator
Inspection
Aspect
Spectacular

Triangle

Tripod

Triple

Tricycle

Monday

Holiday

Birthday

Friday

Circle

Circuit

Circulate

Circumference

Centimetre

Century

Cent

Centipede

Scribe

Scribble

Script

Describe

Scriptures

Exit

Expel

Expense

External

Portable

Import

Export

Transport

Can you help the aliens to work out what the
root words mean for each of the piles of cards?

You are led to the next room:

The word building office

Here, the aliens have split up words into bits like this:

Prefix   **Base word**   **Suffix**

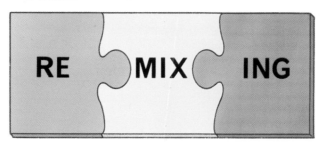

RE   MIX   ING

The aliens have discovered that you can mix and match a lot of these bits together. Prefixes and suffixes will fit on many words. Examples of prefixes are:

Prefixes are easy to spell. You just add them to the front of words.

Pre + cooked = precooked

Re + play = replay

Dis + satisfied = dissatisfied

Dis + appear = disappear

The aliens have one very large collection of prefixes:

The no words

Prefixes that say no:

    UN (e.g. Unlikely)

    DIS (e.g. Disappear)

    ANTI (e.g. Anti-clockwise)

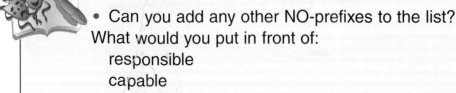

- Can you add any other NO-prefixes to the list?
  What would you put in front of:
      responsible
      capable
      compose?

- Can you think of examples for each NO prefix?

- Can you see why dissatisfied has two Ss, but disappear has only one?

Suffixes are easy to spell.

You add them to the end of the word, but take care if the last letter of the word is a Y or an E.

Examples of suffixes are:

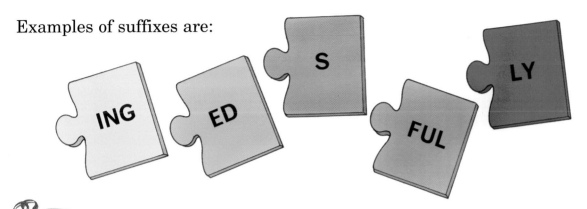

• Can you use these lists to work out the rules about changing letters when you add a suffix
  – to ordinary words
  – to words ending in E
  – to words ending in Y?

Ordinary words

wonder	quick	eat	truth	kind	jump	help	slow	meet

Words ending in E

care	time	shine	hope	rare	file	grace	wise	wipe

Words ending in Y

beauty	happy	carry	plenty	merry	buy	pity	tidy	try

FUL	LY	ING
wonderful	quickly	eating
truthful	kindly	jumping
helpful	slowly	meeting
careful	timely	shining
hopeful	rarely	filing
graceful	wisely	wiping
beautiful	happily	carrying
plentiful	merrily	buying
pitiful	tidily	trying

There are two piles of words that really puzzle the aliens:

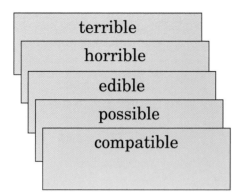

terrible
horrible
edible
possible
compatible

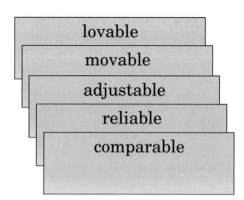

lovable
movable
adjustable
reliable
comparable

Why do some words end in IBLE and others end in ABLE?

Some people can hear the difference. Some people remember the look of the word.

But there are two other ways of working it out.

• Look at the piles and see if you can work out the rules.

HELP

IBLE AND ABLE

1 Look at the root of the word.
  Is the root a word you know?
  If it is, does it end in IBLE or ABLE? If the root is meaningless, does it end in IBLE or ABLE?

2 Look at the word. Are you ABLE to do it?

A key exception to these rules are words ending in S. Words ending in S usually take the suffix IBLE.

Finally…

What happens if you forget a rule?

Easy!

Think of the words you do know, and work it out again.

(For example, if you know horrible and lovable, you can work out the ABLE and IBLE rule for yourself.)

THE WORD MUSEUM

In the next room, the aliens have set up
a museum of words and their history:

SUNDAY
A day of the week.
Named after the sun,
which was once treated as a god.

• Other days of the week are named after Gods.
Can you find out who they were?

CHILDREN   SHEEP   MICE
These words do not add S to make
them plural.
They are very old words from the days
before S was used.

• Can you think of any other examples of such words?

PIZZA   SOUFFLÉ   BLANCMANGE
Words used by the English which have
been borrowed from other countries.

• Where does the word pizza come from?

• Where do the words soufflé and blancmange come from?

• Can you think of any other examples?

HOLIDAY

People used to get a day off on Saints' days.

- Can you work out how the word holiday came about?

KNOW KNOCK

In the old days, people said the K out loud. Then it fell out of fashion. People thought it was rather common to say it that way.

- Can you think of any other silent K words?

- Can you think of any other letters which are often silent?

HELP

A good way to remember silent letters in your spelling is to sometimes say the word to yourself exactly as it is spelt.

PRIMROSE

Primrose was so called because it flowered very early in the year.

- Can you work out what **prim** means?
  Think of other words beginning with **prim** to help you.

- Can you give the aliens any other words to include in their museum?

WORD COLLECTION POINT

You are about to leave the alien spaceship to go home to Earth. In the last room, the aliens are working out the best ways to learn the new spellings they have collected.

As you are leaving, they give you their tips. Read them carefully and decide if any of them can help you with spellings you find difficult.

By Sound

- Say the word out loud, slowly

- Try breaking it into bits

- Learn tricky words by sounding out even the silent letters

By Look

- Look at the word carefully

- Colour over the tricky bit

- Cover it over and try to remember it

- Test yourself every day (use a friend, or a tape recorder to keep a list of words you find tricky)

- Put up a big poster of your key spellings by your bed

By Rules

- Learn the rules

- Build words up bit by bit

- Learn groups of similar words together (e.g. here, there, where)

- Think of words you do know and work it out from those

- Learn a key word to remind you of others

By a Trick

- First letters (e.g. Big Elephants Can Always Use Some Eggs = BECAUSE)

- Words within words (e.g. There's **a rat** in sep**arat**e)

WHAT DID YOU LEARN?

In this unit you have looked at how words make sentences and how they are spelt. Now ask yourself the following questions:

1 What is a noun? Give an example.
  What is a verb? Give an example.
  What is an adjective? Give an example.

2 What does a preposition do? Give an example.
  What does a connective do? Give an example.

3 Write down two rules about the order of words in a sentence.

4 Which three punctuation marks can you use to end a sentence?

5 What are the two main uses of the comma?

6 What is a prefix? What is a suffix?

7 What are the meanings of the prefixes RE, TRI, and SCRIB?

8 When you add a suffix, you have to watch out for words ending in E or Y. Why?

HOW DID YOU DO?

1 How have you gone about learning spellings in the past? Have you found any new ways of learning them in this unit?

2 What has been your biggest problem with punctuation in the past? Find a reading book and look at how writers tackle punctuation. See if you can work out the right way to do it.

3 What do you usually do with work that your teacher has marked? Discuss in your group or with your teacher what you can do to learn from the marking.

UNIT FIVE

Storytelling

We can all tell stories. In this unit you will discover the ingredients of a good story. You will also look at the ways a storyteller weaves a gripping tale. You will develop your skills as:

SPEAKERS AND LISTENERS

by listening to storytellers telling their tales

by sharing and talking about ideas with others

by becoming a storyteller yourself

READERS

by reading extracts from stories from different cultures and countries

by sorting out muddled words, phrases and sentences

WRITERS

by making notes to organise and plan your ideas

by writing your own descriptions

by completing unfinished sentences and stories

Turn the page to find out about different kinds of stories.
You will learn about folk tales, fables, legends and myths ...

STORIES AND STORYTELLERS

We read stories in newspapers and books. We watch stories on television. We also tell our own stories, for example, to our friends on the telephone or when we meet up with them. Our parents might have told us stories when we were young.

There are lots of different kinds of stories. In this unit you will be looking at:

Folk Tales

Fables

Legends

Myths

Folk Tale – a short story about ordinary people. It might include magic.

Fable – a story which is made up to give an example of why a person should behave in a certain way. We say it has a 'moral'. This type of story can use animals as characters.

Legend – a longer story usually about a person who existed in the past, such as Robin Hood. It might be true, but nobody really knows.

Myth – a story about a supernatural being (such as a god or a horse with wings). It was once believed to be true because it explained how the world came to be as it is.

- Listen to the first story, *The Mysterious Traveller*.

- When you have finished listening, make a list of the things you remember from the story. Use these headings to help you.

  1 The worst thing that happened

  2 Something one of the characters said

  3 The moment in the story you enjoyed most

  4 When you guessed what was going to happen in the end

- What has helped you remember the story?

- What kind of story is *The Mysterious Traveller*? Refer to the glossary (left).

- Draw a picture of the setting in which the story takes place.

HELP

The setting tells you where the story takes place. It could be the background scenery or it could be the time of day. It could even tell you the year or century.

The background scenery, the time and the characters in the story probably helped you remember what happened. These things are important when you tell a story. On the next page, you will find a set of rules for storytellers.

RULES
FOR TELLING A STORY

1 Never learn a story word for word. Remember it as a sequence of pictures in your mind.

2 Every story has a beginning, a middle and an end.

3 Make the ending of your story as good as the opening.

4 You can make a story come alive by using words which describe what something is like.

5 The way you tell a story can make it come alive.

6 You should hold your audience's attention all the way to the end.

SEQUENCING STORIES

1 Never learn a story word for word. Remember it as a sequence of pictures in your mind.

In telling a story, a storyteller always follows a sequence.

• Listen to Story Two, *Oona, Finn and Cuchulain.* While you are listening, make a list of all the things that happen in the story. Set your work out like this:

TIME	ACTION
The Beginning	Giant Finn McCool is afraid of the biggest giant of them all, Cuchulain.
The Middle 1	Cuchulain is coming to fight him and he knows Cuchulain will win.
2	Oona, Finn's wife, has a plan.
3	
4	
5	
6	
The End	

- Design a **storyboard** for the story *Oona, Finn and Cuchulain* (see the Help Box below).

- Copy the boxes below. Underneath each box write down your points in order.

- Now draw a picture in the box which shows what is happening in the story. The first two have been done for you.

- You may like to storyboard this story as if it is told by one of the characters. Think about how they would tell what happened.

2 Every story has a beginning, a middle and an end.

Now that you've made a storyboard, you need to look more
closely at what goes into each part of the story. It's easy to divide
a story into three sections: a beginning, a middle and an end.

BEGINNINGS

The very beginning of a story is called the 'opening'.
Look at the story openings below:

> Once upon a time
> when all big folks were
> wee ones and all lies
> were true…

> Once upon a time and
> twice upon a time and
> all times together as
> ever I heard tell of…

> One fine day long ago, when
> birds did talk and beasts
> did sing and grasshoppers
> did spit tobacco…

> Once upon a time, and a very good
> time it was, though it wasn't in my
> time, nor in your time, nor anyone
> else's time, but sometime…

> Before the beginning, in
> times before time…

> Once upon a time, somewhere
> in the lands that lie between
> the sunrise and the sunset,
> there lived…

> On the far side of the shining sands,
> where the sound of one step upon the
> shining white grains can be heard a
> hundred miles away…

> Many snows in
> the past…

- With a partner, discuss which openings you like best and why.

- Try saying each of them aloud. Do they sound different from each other? Why?

- Now make up some openings of your own.

- Look in books of folk tales, fables, myths and legends and make a collection of story openings that you find.

- Write them out and illustrate them.

- Put up a display in your classroom of all the different openings you've made or collected.

HELP

You could try a Once Upon a time… style. You could try an opening where time is measured by moons, suns, daylight, darkness or seasons.

ENDINGS

You are now going to look at different ways storytellers end their stories.

3 Make the ending of your story as good as the opening.

There are many ways of ending a story. Your last lines should be ones that your listeners will enjoy and remember.
Look at these examples of story endings. They come from different folk tales.

...*This is my tale, I've told it, and in your hands I leave it.*

...*And that is all there is to the story; you can take it from me.*

...*Such strange things sometimes still happen.*

...*And that is the end of it.*

...*So that's how* ...

...*And the mouth of the last man to tell this tale is still warm.*

...*Only, as time went by, pedlars and storytellers became rarer and rarer, so that, nowadays, almost nobody remembers this tale.*

...*And that is why, to this very day*...

- Which of the endings do you like best and why?

- With a partner, read the endings aloud. How do they sound?

- Now make up some endings of your own.

- Try out your endings by saying them to your partner, then choose the ones that sound best.

- Look in books of folk tales, fables, myths and legends and make a collection of story endings that you find. Write them out and illustrate them.

- Put up a display in your classroom of all the different endings you've made or collected.

HELP

You could try a 'happy ever after' ending…

You could try a 'cliffhanger' ending – one which leaves the listener wondering what happens next…

MAKING A STORY COME ALIVE

4. You can make a story come alive by using words which describe what something is like.

You have a really good opening to grab the listener's attention. You have an ending that keeps the listeners hooked until the very end. Now you need the middle.

A storyteller helps to make a story come alive in the minds of the listeners by describing what characters, objects, places and events look like or sound like. This can be done in many ways:

- by using different voices for different characters
- by using words that sound as if they come from the time when the story is set
- by speaking slowly or speeding up depending on what is happening in the story.

- Copy out and complete the sentences below:

A really good opening to a story is important because…

A really good ending to a story is important because…

A storyteller uses different voices for…

A storyteller can speak…

DESCRIBING THINGS

Look at the extract below. It is from a story called 'From Tiger to Anansi'. Anansi, the main character, is a 'trickster'. He appears in lots of stories told in West Africa and the Carribean. He is part man, part spider.

In this story, Anansi is set a task by Tiger. He has to bring Snake to Tiger. He has to bring him alive within six days. Tiger knows this would be really hard for Anansi to do because Snake is very sly.

- This extract is missing some words.

- Read the extract aloud to a partner. How does it sound when some of the words are missing?

- On a copy of this page, fill in the blank spaces. Use the Help Box to help you choose the best words.

- Read the extract aloud, to a partner. Try if a few times to make the descriptions sound effective. How does it sound?

- Try other words in some of the blank spaces. What descriptions can you make? How does the story sound with different descriptions?

On Wednesday Anansi had another idea. He made a _____ hole in the ground. He made the _____ sides of the hole impossible to climb by spreading _____ grease all over them. Right at the bottom he put some _____ bananas – just the sort that Snake loved. Then he hid in a _____ bush beside the _____ road and waited. Snake came crawling down the _____ path towards the _____ river. He was _____ hungry and _____ thirsty. He could smell the _____ bananas and followed his nose to the _____ hole where he saw them right at the _____ bottom. Snake saw that the _____ sides of the hole were slippery. First he wrapped his _____ tail tightly round the _____ trunk of a nearby tree. Then he stretched his _____ body as far as it would go and reached down into the hole. He ate the _____ bananas. When he was finished he pulled himself up by his tail and slid contentedly away towards the _____ river to drink. He was _____ satisfied. But Anansi was not satisfied. He had lost his bananas and he had lost Snake too.

HELP

Word bank

slippery long ripe deep hot tasty

steep very thick scaly dusty cool

coarse delicious

- You can use some of these words more than once.
- You can use more than one word in a blank space.

The words which you have just used are all **adjectives**. Adjectives are words which describe nouns. For storytellers adjectives are very useful because they help make the story come alive. They help create a picture in your mind.

For example:

First he wrapped his scaly tail tightly round the thick trunk of a nearby tree.

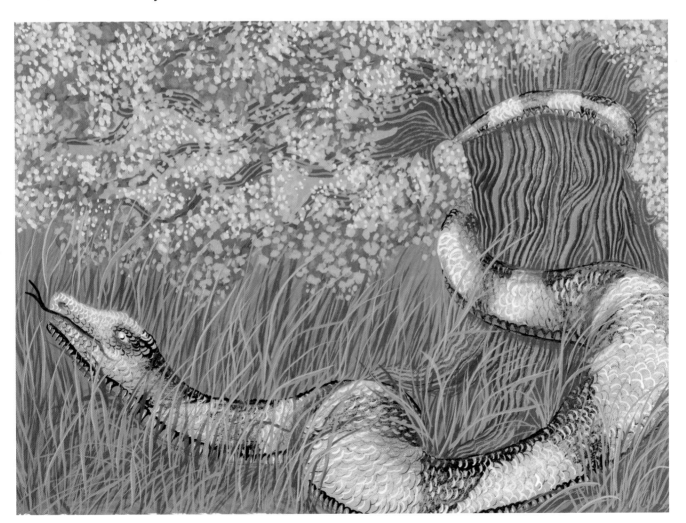

MIX AND MATCH

Below is a list of adjectives and nouns.

- On a copy of this page, cut around the nouns and adjectives.
- Put the adjectives next to the nouns which they best describe.

HELP

There are no right answers for this activity – you need to choose adjectives and nouns which sound right together. Answer the question below to help you think about this.

- Which sounds best: 'bold village', 'bright village' or 'deserted village'?

Adjectives	Nouns
crafty	scoundrel
jealous	castle
loyal	star
cold	teeth
pearly	sun
deserted	village
deadly	traveller
golden	knight
bright	servant
weary	poison

• Now write two sentences using the adjectives and nouns you have matched together. For example:
The crafty scoundrel upset the jealous knight.

• Compare your sentences with a partner. How were they different? What effects do different words have?

HOW A STORYTELLER WORKS

5 The way you tell a story can make it come alive.

- Listen to Hugh Lupton of The Company of Storytellers, or your teacher, telling the extract below from *Sir Gawain and the Green Knight*.

- Read the extract aloud to a partner. Try it a few times to make it sound effective.

- With your partner, practise saying 'green' in lots of different ways. Now practise saying 'great green'. What makes these words sound good together?

- Think up a character: it could be a friend or relative or you could invent someone.

- Use word patterns to write a short description of this character.

…and this knight was green. His hair was green, his face was green, his great green beard spread across a green chest, green legs, green sandals on his feet and his horse was green from the tips of his ears to the hooves on his feet.

   And in one hand the green knight was carrying a great green axe and in the other hand a bunch of holly bobbing with red berries. And the eyes in the green knight's head were as red as the holly berries…

HELP

Grouping words which sound similar makes the words form a pattern. Word patterns can be made:

- by repeating words
- by repeating sounds
- by using words which rhyme

Word patterns help you remember a story. They can help make the story come alive in your mind.

Word patterns help to make a story sound good, but there are other kinds of words which can make a story come alive. These words are called verbs and adverbs.

HELP

Verb = a word which describes an action

Adverb = a word which describes how an action happened

For example: The Snake slid contentedly away...

- What did the snake do?
- How did he do it?

- Now listen to the second extract from the story, *Sir Gawain and the Green Knight.* Something that makes this part of the story come alive is the way the storyteller uses verb and adverbs.

- When you have listened, read the extract below. There are two verbs where there should only be one. Choose the best verbs and list them.

- Compare your list with a partner's. Did you choose the same verbs? If not, discuss your reasons for your choice.

- There is one adverb in this extract. Can you find it?

...the head rolled from the Green Knight's shoulders. And it

rolled
hopped across the floor of the hall, and it

rolled
dropped under the

Round Table and there were the knights of the Round Table

kicking
pushing it with their feet to the one side and the other side. But,

the body of the Green Knight, it didn't falter or

run
fall it stayed

steady. And then, slowly it got to its feet, and slowly it

dashed
walked

across the floor of the hall until it came to the Round Table and

there it

stooped
stopped and with one of its arms

stretched
reached beneath the

table it felt the hair of its own head between its fingers. And

clutching
grabbing the hair of its head it lifted the head high above the

shoulders and it

turned
spun the head round until the two red eyes

were looking straight at Sir Gawain.

CREATING PICTURES

- Read the sentences below. The second half of each sentence has been mixed up!

- On a copy of this page, cut round the dotted lines. Match the first half of each sentence with the correct second half.

Then on the fourth day he spotted a fish shining like…	…the moon, and big enough to feed a village.
He began to move with the music, fluttering his arms like…	…a deer pawing the snow.
He stamped his feet like…	…a lily on her lips.
It was a feather that shone bright red and gold like…	…the wings of a raven.
They said her smile blossomed like…	…a wild overgrown garden.
It's hair was thick and tangled like…	…a tiny tongue of flame.

HELP

These descriptions are called similes. This means that you can describe something by comparing it with something else. To do this you use the word 'like'. For example:

'he spotted a fish shining like the moon'.

The storyteller is saying the fish looks like the moon. So the fish is shiny and white.

• In a pair, try out the similes you've made by saying them to each other. Choose the one that sounds best. Why did you like it?

• Now make up a simile! Here are some ideas to start you off.
The old witch's fingers were like...
The deep river flowed fast like...
The clouds in the sky looked like...
The ticking of time was like...
The knight's armour shone like...

You can make your simile exciting:
The angry giant's voice roared like a clap of thunder.

Or you can make your simile funny:
The singing voice of the princess sounded like the croak of a frog.

• Draw a picture of your simile. Write your simile underneath the picture.

• You could make a class display of all your similes.

THE LAST WORDS

6 You should hold your audience's attention all the way to the end.

Listen carefully to Story Three, *Vasilissa the Fair.*

There has been some technical problem with the recording so the final part of the story has gone missing! You must provide the ending. Follow the ideas below to make a really good ending to the story.

Step 1

Choose **how** you want to end the story. Here are some different kinds of ending:

- Happy ever after.
  Who would be happy at the end? How?

- A sad ending.
  Someone might die or be driven away.

- A cliffhanger.
  Have Vasilissa's problems been solved? Look back at p114 to remind yourself about cliffhangers.

Step 2

Talk through these ideas with a partner. Now both tell your ending to another pair in your class.

HELP

Here are some points to remember when you make up your ending.

- Will Vasilissa's stepmother and stepsisters be pleased to see her or will they be surprised that she has come back?

- What will the stepmother and stepsisters do when they see the lighted skull?

- What will happen to the lighted skull when it sees the stepmother and stepsisters?

- Will Baba-Yaga come into the story any more?

- Will Vasilissa's special doll be important?

Now that you have told your ending you will be able to hear the ending told by the storyteller – it has been found on another part of the tape.

- Listen carefully to the storyteller's ending.

- Was your ending the same?
- What was different about your ending?

The covers below are from some collections of stories.

In pairs, discuss the following:

- Which cover do you like the best? Why?
- Do the covers tell you what the stories will be about?
- Which cover makes you want to read the stories?

On your own:

- Draw a front cover for *Vasilissa the Fair.* Think carefully about what the picture on the front will show. Will it make others want to read the story?

MAKING STORIES

You have listened to storytellers tell stories. You know what makes a good beginning, middle and end. You know how storytellers use words to make their stories come alive. Now it's your turn to be a storyteller!

MINI-TALES

We all know something that has happened to a friend. Maybe something has happened to you.

Think about a time when:

- you were really frightened
- someone gave you a surprise party
- you had a lucky escape
- someone played a trick on you.

- Listen to the tale by Kevin Farrow, a year 7 student, about a time when a ghost came to visit him.

- When you have listened to the story write one sentence for each of the questions below.

  1 How did it start?

  2 What happened?

  3 Who did it happen to?

  4 When and where did it happen?

  5 How did it happen?

  6 Who else was involved?

  7 How did it end?

- Choose one word from each of these sentences. You now have seven words. This is your **bone pattern** (see the Help Box opposite).

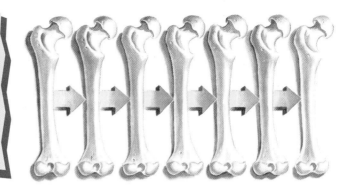

HELP

For every story you wish to tell, always make a **bone pattern** of seven words. This will help you remember your story. It will help you remember the sequence of your story. Each word will tell you what comes next.

TELLING YOUR OWN MINI-TALE

- Choose one of the story ideas on the last page.

- Write one sentence for each of these questions.

1 How will it start?

2 What will it happen?

3 Who will it happen to?

4 When and where will it happen?

5 How will it happen?

6 Who else will be involved?

7 How will it end?

- Choose one word from each of your sentences. You now have seven words which form your bone pattern.

- Try to remember the words of your bone pattern. They will remind you of what happens in your story.

- Practise telling your story to a partner.

- Now swap partners and tell your mini-tale. Listen to your partner's mini-tale.

HELP

- Tell your mini-tale clearly so that your partner can follow your story.

- Listen carefully to your partner's tale.

- You can swap tales as many times as you like.

- You can collect tales from friends and relatives.

- Tell as many tales as you can to other friends. Get them to exchange their tales for yours.

WHAT DID YOU LEARN?

You have listened to stories being told and learned the rules of storytelling. You have told a story and become a storyteller yourself. Now ask yourself the following questions.

1 What makes a good start to a story?

2 What makes a good end to a story?

3 What are nouns and adjectives?

4 How can you use them to describe things?

5 What are similes?

6 How can you use them to describe things?

7 What tips can you give someone who has never told a story?

HOW DID YOU DO?

1 Which part of this unit did you enjoy most and why? Can you explain what you liked about it?

2 In what ways is this work better than work you have done before?

3 If you had to go back to one section and do it again, which one would you choose and what would you do differently?

4 What would you most like to improve about your storytelling? What do you need to do to improve this skill?

Autobiography

They say everybody has a story to tell. In this unit you will complete tasks which will make you think about the details of your life. The tasks will help you collect together information about yourself and you will plan, write and talk about your own autobiography.

You will develop your skills as:

SPEAKERS AND LISTENERS

by talking about yourself
by describing important events in your life
by promoting your own autobiography

READERS

by reading autobiographies written by others
by selecting information from different sources

WRITERS

by completing short tasks to help you think about your own life
by writing the first chapter of your own autobiography

You probably know some facts about yourself – your date of birth, your nationality. But there are lots of ingredients that make you different from everyone else…

WHAT IS AN AUTOBIOGRAPHY?

Auto (greek) means self

Bio (greek) means life

Graphy (greek) a form of writing

(Collins English Dictionary)

A biography is the story of a person's life.

An autobiography is the story of a person's life written by that person.

Here is an extract from Billy Connolly's autobiography:

There used to be these air raid shelters all over the place and we would leap around on top of them. There was the 'Shelter-to-Shelter' jump, which was legendary. They were like mountaineering passes and routes: the White Patch, the Wee Sui and the Big Sui, which was short for suicide.

The Day I jumped the Big Sui…oh, the feeling. It was like suddenly maturing, like the Indian brave's initiation rites, passing into manhood. And being able to jump the Big Sui was no mean feat. Maybe it was because I was a wee boy, but it seemed like one hell of a distance to jump. It was from the top of the air raid shelter, across a void with railings in the middle of it that divided one back court from another, and then you had to land on top of this midden with a sloped roof. You had to stop dead there or you were right off over the other side.

Geordie Sinclair's attempt at it I remember well. Geordie was wearing these boots that a lot of the boys wore at the time. Parish boots they were called; all studded and tackety and funny. And he was running like a madman, like a dervish, across the shelter, then leapt into the air and Did the Big Sui. But when he hit the midden, he went into an incredibly fast slide and ended up in mid-air in a sitting position, with a trail of sparks coming from his studs. Landed right on his arse in the back green.

Billy Connolly

- What might Billy Connolly call this extract?
- What might he call the whole autobiography?

- In pairs or small groups, talk about what you would expect to read in an autobiography.

Here is what Roald Dahl has to say about his. It is called *Boy:*

An autobiography is a book a person writes about his own life and it is usually full of all sorts of boring details.

This is not an autobiography. I would never write a history of myself. On the other hand, throughout my young days at school and just afterwards a number of things happened to me that I have never forgotten.

None of these things is important, but each of them made such a tremendous impression on me that I have never been able to get them out of my mind. Each of them, even after a lapse of fifty and sometimes sixty years, has remained seared on my memory.

I didn't have to search for any of them. All I had to do was skim them off the top of my consciousness and write them down.

Some are funny. Some are painful. Some are unpleasant. I suppose that is why I have always remembered them so vividly. All are true.

R.D.

- Look carefully at the covers and titles of the autobiographies opposite.

- In pairs, talk about why these writers might have chosen these titles for their autobiographies.

- Can you match these writers to their autobiographies?

Michael Barrymore *Long Walk to Freedom*

Benazir Bhutto *To Be Honest with You*

Nelson Mandela *Back in Business*

Linford Christie *Daughter of the East*

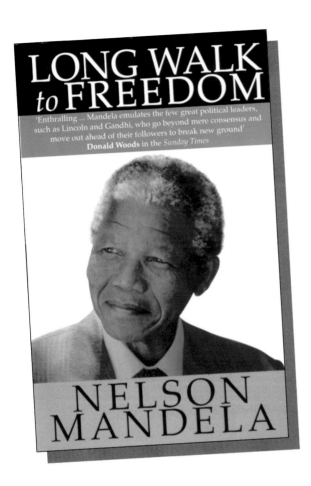

LONG WALK to FREEDOM

'Enthralling ... Mandela emulates the few great political leaders, such as Lincoln and Gandhi, who go beyond mere consensus and move out ahead of their followers to break new ground'
Donald Woods in the *Sunday Times*

NELSON MANDELA

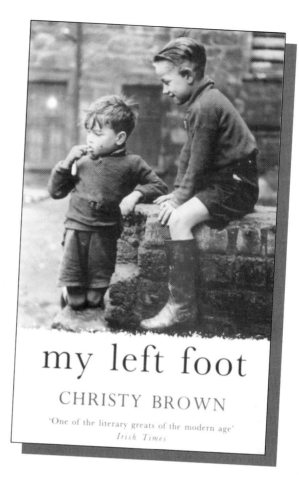

my left foot

CHRISTY BROWN

'One of the literary greats of the modern age'
Irish Times

Roald Dahl

'Throughout my young days at school and just afterwards a number of things happened to me... Some are funny. Some are painful. Some are unpleasant ... All are 'true'
– Roald Dahl

BOY

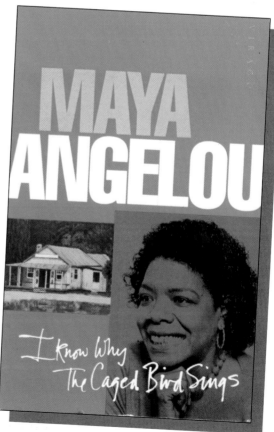

MAYA ANGELOU

I Know Why The Caged Bird Sings

Think about words that describe how you feel. Look at the picture below to help you.

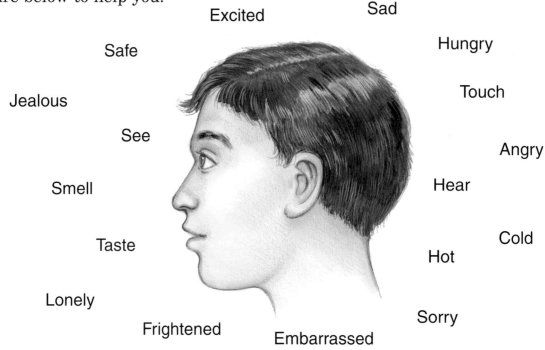

Excited Sad

Safe Hungry

Jealous Touch

See Angry

Smell Hear

Taste Cold

Hot

Lonely Sorry

Frightened Embarrassed

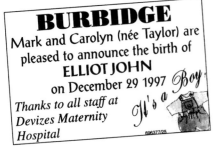

• Write a paragraph describing a time when you had one of the feelings described above.

Begin your writing with this title:
A Time when I was Feeling…

BIRTH ANNOUNCEMENTS

Parents put Birth Announcements in newspapers.

Look at these Birth Announcements.

BURBIDGE
Mark and Carolyn (née Taylor) are pleased to announce the birth of
ELLIOT JOHN
on December 29 1997
It's a Boy!
Thanks to all staff at Devizes Maternity Hospital
696637/25

It's a GIRL **MacARTHUR**
To Ian and Jackie (nee Marsh) a daughter
Ailsa Isabelle
(9lb 2oz)
born December 19, 1997, at Kingston Hospital Surrey. First grandchild for Pete and Judy Marsh.
696380/3/27

GILES
Sarah and Edward
are delighted to announce the birth of their daughter
ELSBETH ROSE
on November 26, 1997
A sister for Rachael, Sam and Henry.
684674/51/22

• Here is a blank Birth Announcement.
On a copy fill in your own details.

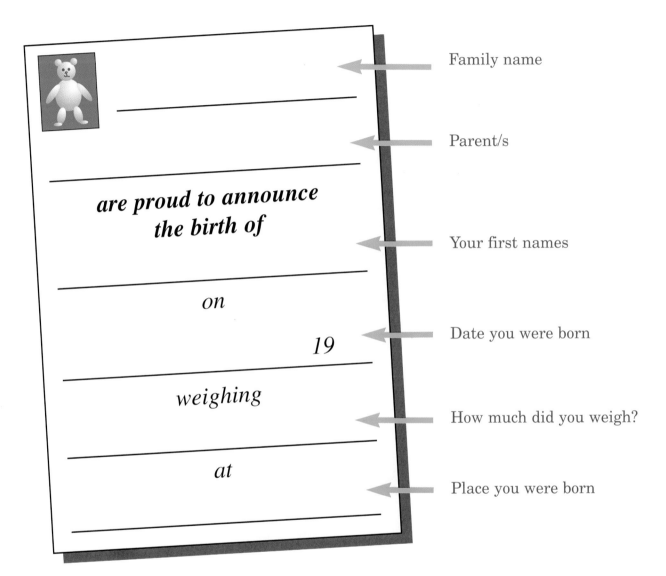

are proud to announce the birth of — Your first names

on

19 — Date you were born

weighing — How much did you weigh?

at — Place you were born

Family name

Parent/s

INFORMATION ABOUT YOU

Think of all the information which has been written about you.
For example, medical records, school reports, letters, diaries...

• Research some of this information to find the facts
about you. Record what you find on a grid, like this:

FACTS ABOUT ME		
Type of information	*Who reads it?*	*Why was it written?*
School report	*Me, parents, a friend, a teacher...*	*To describe my work and progress at school*

One way of gathering information about yourself is to ask others what they think. You can imagine what they would say or actually ask them.

• What would the following people say about you?
Write a sentence for each of them.

My parents would say…
My best friend would say…
My teacher would say…

• Can you think of any more people? Add their comments to your list.

My form mistress at Milford, Mrs Olwyn Joyce, was heard despairingly telling my parents that she wished the school had been built in a traditional style rather than with modern, panoramic windows. Being easily distracted by the sight and sound of a bouncing ball, I was forever staring out of the window watching the other classes playing games and wishing I was out there with them.

Ian Botham, *My Autobiography*

On the next page are extracts from the autobiographies of two famous people. Read them carefully to yourself.

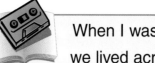

My first memories are of living in Kingston, Jamaica, in a really big house. At least that's the way it seemed to me. I lived there until I was seven and I have been back since. I now realize that the house was not as large as I thought it was. In fact, I'm a bit disillusioned because many of the things which were around when I was a boy have changed a great deal. But none of that can take away the wonderful memories I have of life in Jamaica.

...

The first time it started to snow, I ran outside and opened my mouth to catch it. I had never seen snow before and knew nothing about it. Eventually my fingers went numb, then my toes. The lowest temperatures in Jamaica were usually in the sixties. I'd never felt the cold before and this was a big shock to my system. I really cried. I just didn't understand what was happening.

Linford Christie, *To Be Honest with You*

When I was five years old and we lived across the street from a little grocery store, and Mother allowed me to go over there all by myself (which meant, of course, that she would stand there, and make sure all the traffic had subsided, and then, like a track coach, scream alright, go! and while I was going she would scream run! run! like it was the end of the world. I did not cross a street without her until I was nine years old).

When I came back and handed Mother her purchase she noticed I'd been given $1 too much in change, and decided to educate me as to the wise and crucial ways of being honest and god-fearing and right thinking and all, but because it was very cold outside, I refused to go back. Mother then drilled into me that our heavenly father was watching and would like it if I took back the dollar. Thus properly induced into religious ecstasy, turning to return the excess loot, I slipped on the ice and all of my upper teeth went cleanly and fully through my lip; I was rushed to the hospital, laid on a table, covered with a sheet from head to toe and underwent ninety minutes of surgery.

Roseanne Barr, *My Life as a Woman*

You have just read some earliest memories from two famous people.
Use their experiences to help   mplete your own timeline of events.

TIMELINE OF EVENTS

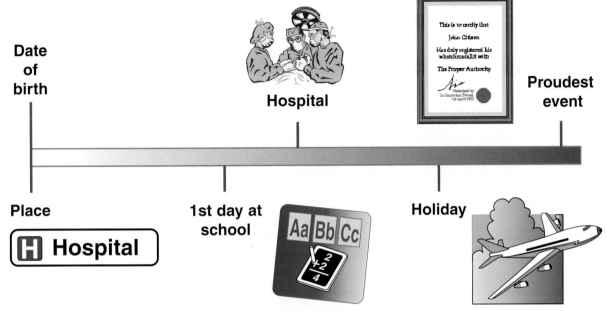

| Date of birth | | Hospital | | Proudest event |

Place

H Hospital

1st day at school

Holiday

One way to select an early memory to write about is to collect ideas. Try this:

1 On a sheet of paper write 'my early memories' like this:

> my earliest memories

2 Use 'branches' coming out of the bubble to jot down anything you remember from your early childhood.
Then write further 'branches' from these as you remember other details for each memory. Here is an example:

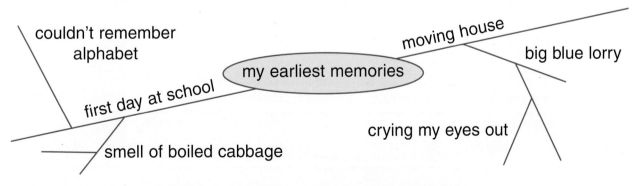

couldn't remember alphabet

moving house

big blue lorry

my earliest memories

first day at school

crying my eyes out

smell of boiled cabbage

3 Now choose *one* memory to write 5 to 10 lines about. Begin *'One of my earliest memories is...'*.

WHAT DO YOU LOOK LIKE?

Make a wanted poster which includes a picture and written description of yourself. What crime have you committed? Not doing the washing up, arguing with your brother/sister, not handing in homework spilling gravy on your English exercise book…

FAME AT LAST!

You have made it! You are famous, a celebrity. Your adoring fans want to know all about you. What will you be famous for?

- Sport?

- Acting?

- Singing?

- Politics?

YOUR FACTFILE

You have to send out information to the members of your fan club. You will need a factfile. On the following pages are three factsheets for you to fill in to make up your factfile.

- Begin your factfile by filling in your details on a copy of the factsheet below.

THE FACTS ABOUT ME
My full name is
I was born
My first school was
My school now is
My best friend at school is
There are ———— in my family. They are:
My favourite food is
My favourite TV programme is
My favourite song is
My favourite animal is

Here is an example of the fact file of a TV celebrity. Are there any details here which you can include in your fact file? Is there anything you would keep top secret?

top secrets

It's not all sticky-back plastic and yoghurt pots on Blue Peter you know!

☺ **What animals are you most scared of and why?**
"Giant water turtles because I came across one when I was swimming once. It was huge – at least the size of a garage!" **We've told him a million times not to exaggerate!**

☺ **Who don't you swear in front of, and why not?**
"I would never swear on air because I'd get the sack!"

☺ **What kind of pants are you wearing at the moment?**
"Marks & Spencer paisley patterned boxer shorts."

☺ **What's the most imperfect part of your body?**
"My love handles!"

☺ **Have you ever two-timed anyone and, if so, were you caught?**
"Oooh, I couldn't possibly say!" **Yeah, you could!**

☺ **Have you ever worried that you weren't normal?**
"No – doesn't everyone wear paisley patterned underwear?!"

☺ **Name someone who has made you cry. What did they do?**
"My mum – when she used to tell me off when I was little!"

☺ **Who makes you all hot and bothered?**
"Helen Baxendale." **(Actress who starred in** *Cardiac Arrest*)

☺ **What's your most anti-social habit?**
"I mop up the left-over gravy on my plate with a thick slice of white bread."

☺ **Who is the ugliest person you can think of?**
"Anybody who wears those trendy yellow-tinted glasses!!"

☺ **Were you ever bullied?**
"No, I was lucky enough not to have been picked on at school."

Cheeky blighter **Marie-Claire Giddings**

Blue Peter's Richard

Now you are famous, your opinion can influence others.

• Copy and complete the factsheet below.

My opinions on...		
Rules	1	
	2	
	3	
Homework	1	
	2	
	3	
Fashion	1	
	2	
	3	
Pets	1	
	2	
	3	

- Think about:

  – your feelings

  – your hopes for the future

  – what you want people to know and what you don't
    want them to know!

- Copy and complete the factsheet below.

FEELINGS
What makes you happy?
What makes you sad?
What makes you angry?

HOPES FOR THE FUTURE
Where will you go from here?
In 1 years' time?
In 5 years' time?
In 10 years' time?

GIVING AWAY YOUR SECRETS
What was the funniest thing that ever happened to you?
What was the worst thing that ever happened to you?
What was the most embrassing thing that ever happened to you?

Here are some examples of autobiographical writing by students in Year 7. They have each written the first chapter of their autobiography about their earliest memories.

● Read each extract carefully and give each a chapter title.

When I was about 2 my dad took me to the Oasis and took me down the slides. We got to the last one, the biggest one with a shower of water half way down and when we got there the water came down and I thought it was leeking and I was going to die.

When I was 4 my nan died and I cannot remember her at all. All I can remember is that she was really nice and kind and that she died of breast cancer. I didn't understand. I can't remember my first day at school but I can remember my first time swimming with the school because I was sent out for shouting. I remember looking at the grey brick wall and all my friends swimming and laughing.

When I was two I was at playschool.
I was standing in the middle of the
room painting quietly. There was alot of
noise but it was all blocked out all I could
hear was ~~a~~ one of the helpers telling us
to be quiet. My picture was ~~ver~~ very
colourful. It was of my house and there
were trees and flowers. I watched my
paint brush flow from side to side with
bright blue paint then I turned to the yellow
and dunked my brush into the pot
then splated the brush onto my paper in
the corner to make the ~~sun~~ sun. Then I remembered
looking at it in delight. The red house and
blue sky, the yellow sun and green trees.
My first painting and I thought it was
brilliant but then a girl wearing a pink
flowered dress came over to me. She looked
over at my painting and laughed at it.
I felt upset and angry and alone. My eyes
filled with water. I looked at her dress. It
was very clean then I looked at my pot of
water and my brush. I took the brush
and took hold of the dirty grey water in
the pot and threw it at her. Her dress
was now a murky grey colour. I watched
her eyes begin to water. She ran away
and never laughed at me again.

When I was young me and my mum were coming out of the sports centre in Calne. My mum was giving me a piggy back when I was that stupid to let go and I went SPLAT on the floor, My mum rushed me into the sports centre. There was blood dripping every where. My mum was holding my chin so that the blood wouldn't go every where but it did (OH DEAR). She rushed me into the sports centre's mini hospital. They stuck sterer strips on my chin then we went home. A while after that I split my chin open again with a fork so I had to go to hospital again. Then a few months after it healed up I split it open again on the edge of a chair. I have split my chin open six times, once on concrete, once on a chair, twice on our door and twice with a fork and it hurt alot.

It was like being in prison, me and my jailmate my big white teddybear with his clean red t-shirt on, he was about the same size as me but when I sat on him I sank into a mass of white fur. The other toys were as still as ice, died of starvation in this terrible place. It was all quiet, noone around but me and my jailmate. I started running at a slow pace. I was running towards a big brown wooden solid playpen, it was getting bigger and bigger. I stopped. Peering in was a giant with black hair and brown eyes. It was my mum who gave me a drink in a red beaker with two handles and a lid, the lid was on tight. It was blackcurrant. I gave a handle to my jailmate and we shared the drink. My jailmate dribbled. It went down his red t-shirt. I ran towards my playpen bump! I fell back. My jailmate was hurt I gave him a hug. I stood up. The playpen had moved. so I kept bumping into it to make it move.

- You have to select two of the examples to appear in a collection of writing by young people. Which would you choose? Explain your reasons to a partner.

- In pairs, identify the five most important things that make an autobiography interesting to read.

You could think about the following:

- lots of detail
- facts
- clear sentences
- vivid description
- dramatic moments
- emotions
- tells the truth

- Can you think of any others? Make a list of them.

Now it's time to write the first chapter of your own autobiography. Read these opening paragraphs from autobiographies to see how they start.

 Sometime after I was born in Salt Lake City, Utah, all the little babies were sleeping soundly in the nursery except for me, who would scream at the top of my lungs, trying to shove my whole fist into my mouth, wearing all the skin off on the end of my nose. I was put into a tiny restraining jacket to keep my hands away from the wounds.

My mother is fond of this story because to her it illustrates what she regards as my gargantuan appetites and excess anger. I think I was probably just bored.

Six months old. How *dull* everything is. Aunts and uncles would attempt to amuse me by making silly faces at my crib. My grandmother did not bore me, though, because she smelled like bread and pickles.

Roseanne Barr, *My Life as a Woman*

 I was born in the Rotunda Hospital, on June 5th, 1932. There were nine children before me and twelve after me, so I myself belong to the middle group. Out of this total of twenty-two, seventeen lived, four died in infancy, leaving thirteen still to hold the family fort.

Mine was a difficult birth, I am told. Both mother and son almost died. A whole army of relations queued up outside the hospital until the small hours of the morning, waiting for news and praying furiously that it would be good.

After my birth mother was sent to recuperate for some weeks and I was kept in the hospital while she was away. I remained there for some time, without name, for I wasn't baptised until my mother was well enough to bring me to church.

Christy Brown, *My Left Foot*

Using the information you have collected about yourself, write the first chapter of your autobiography. Think about:

– when and were it all started

– your family

– your earliest memory

– your biggest achievement

– your worst memory

– your life so far…

PROMOTING YOUR AUTOBIOGRAPHY

You've written the first chapter about your life. Now people
want to find out more. What questions might they ask?

Tell us about your earliest memories?

Why were you called …

What has been the greatest
moment of your life so far?

How do you get on with
the rest of your family?

What has been your most
embarrassing moment?

- Imagine you are going to interview one of these celebrities. What questions would you ask them?

- Think of five questions for each celebrity.

HELP

Questions, Questions

To be a good interviewer you need to ask the right questions.
You want the answer to your question to be as full as
possible.

The interviewer on the left has asked a 'closed' question. She
receives a one-word answer.

The interviewer on the right has asked an 'open' question.
She receives a full answer.

THE CHAT SHOW

You are going to appear on a chat show to promote your new autobiography and to talk about your life.

- In pairs, decide who will be interviewed and who will be the chat show host.

- **Chat show host**:
Work out the questions you are going to ask. What sort of questions will get the most interesting answer? Write down three questions.

- **Interviewee**: What questions might you be asked? Are there any embarrassing moments in your life you don't want to give away? Think of three events in your life you want to talk about.

- Now get into your roles. Act out your chat show interview.

WHAT DID YOU LEARN?

You have looked at the autobiographies of famous people.
You have written and talked about your own autobiography.
Now ask yourself the following questions:

1 What makes a good autobiography? List four things.

2 Where would you look for information for your autobiography?

3 How do you collect ideas about yourself and your earliest memories?

4 If you were famous, what exciting things would people want to know about you?

5 What is a 'closed' question?
  What is an 'open' question?

6 Why is it better to ask open questions to get the information you want?

7 You have read extracts from the autobiographies of famous people in this unit. Whose autobiography would you most like to read?

HOW DID YOU DO?

1 Which part of this unit did you most enjoy? Can you explain what you liked about it?

2 In what ways is this work better than work you have done before?

3 If you had to go back to one section and do it again which one would you choose? What would you do differently?

4 What would you most like to improve about your autobiography? What do you need to do to improve your skills as an autobiographer?

THE MYSTERIOUS TRAVELLER

Long, long ago on the shores of a lake called Semerwater near Wensleydale in Yorkshire, there stood a small town. The people who lived there had money and land but were selfish and greedy.

One day a poor man came walking through the town. It was October and the lake was grey and ruffled by the cold wind. It would soon be night for the end of the day comes early in the dales.

The traveller had a pack on his back. He shivered in his thin clothes. He knew he must find shelter for the night, but he was sure that someone would take him in.

A man was standing at his open door, the firelight glowing behind him. 'Could I have a bed for the night, friend?' asked the traveller.

'We want no strangers here,' growled the man.

A few cottages farther on, a woman was watching for her husband to come home from work. The traveller was about to ask if he could shelter there but the woman shut the door in his face.

It was the same everywhere; no one welcomed him. At one house the dogs were let loose and he had to run; at another the wife called for her husband to set about him with a stick. In the street a horseman crowded him off the road so that he was spattered with mud. Even the children gathered at the street corner, jeered at him and threw stones.

Tired and hungry, the traveller walked on until he had left the town of unkind folk behind him. He came to a small, grey stone cottage standing by itself. It was so small that it seemed to be tucked into the hillside for shelter. A twisted hawthorn tree hung its scarlet berries over the steep roof.

'Perhaps I shall have better luck here,' thought the traveller and he knocked at the door.

It was opened by a cheerful looking little woman wearing a spotless white apron. 'Come you in,' she said at once. 'You look cold and clemmed.'

'Thank you,' said the traveller gratefully. By the hearth sat an old man. A kettle steamed on the hob and a black cat lay asleep on the mat.

'Sit you down,' said the old man. 'You're welcome to anything we have. 'Tis good to have a visitor. Folk round here are not friendly.'

The traveller shared their supper of oatcakes and milk and when it was done he lay down near the fire, for there was only one room. The wind howled outside but within the little cottage all was peaceful and warm.

In the morning the traveller said farewell and thanked the old man and his wife for the shelter and food they had given him.

The old couple stood at the door and watched him climb the steep path. After a while he paused on the hillside and looked out over the town. It was almost hidden in the rising mist from the grey lake.

Then they saw him stretch out his arms and his long staff until he looked almost like a giant, and they heard him cry in a ringing voice:

'Semerwater rise, Semerwater sink!

Swallow all this town, save the house that gave me food and drink!'

Before the old people's eyes, the lake rose up in great waves, mountain high. Then with a terrible crash the water fell upon the town and hid it from sight. The waves ran hissing up the hillside and stopped just short of the old

couple as they stood trembling with terror.

When they looked around for the traveller, he had disappeared. So had the town with all its wicked people. In its place lay a peaceful unrippled lake, which is there to this day.

OONA AND THE GIANT CUCHULAIN

a tall tale from Ireland

Of all the giants that ever walked the vales of Ireland, the giant Cuchulain was the strongest. With a blow of his mighty fist he could squash a mountain into a cowpat, and he went about the land with one such cowpat in his pockets to scare the other giants.

He scared them all right. They tried to keep out of his way, but he hunted them down, one by one, and beat the living daylights out of them; then they scampered off into the mountains to lick their wounds.

There was one giant, though, that Cuchulain had not yet thrashed and that was Finn MacCool. The reason was simple: Finn MacCool was so afraid of Cuchulain that he kept well out of his way. He even built his house atop a windy mountain to keep a look out all about him; and whenever that mighty giant appeared in the distance, Finn was off like a shot from a cannon, hiding in a bush or a bog or a barrow.

But Finn could not keep his foe at bay forever. And Cuchulain had vowed he would not rest until he had flattened the cowardly Finn. Finn knew the day must come. Do you know how? By sucking his thumb: that made all things clear to him.

So there he was, this Finn, sitting outside his house upon the windy mountain, sucking his great thumb. And, oh dear me! Rushing indoors shivering like a jelly, he cried to his wife Oona, 'Cuchulain is coming this way. And there's no time to escape; my thumb tells me so!'

'What time is he due?' asks Oona.

Finn sucked his thumb again. 'At three o'clock this afternoon. And do you know what he means to do? Squash me flat and carry me in his pocket with his cowpat!'

'Now, now, Finn,' says Oona, 'just leave this to me. Haven't. I pulled you from the mire many times before?'

'Indeed you have,' said Finn. And he stopped his shivering.

In the meantime Oona went down to three friends at the foot of the mountain, and at each house she borrowed an iron griddle. Once home with her three griddles, she baked half a dozen cakes, each as big as a basket; and inside three she put an iron griddle while the dough was soft. Then she placed the cakes in a row upon two shelves: three above, three below, so that she would know which one was which.

At two o'clock she glanced out of the window and spied a speck on the horizon; she guessed it was Cuchulain coming. Straightaway she dressed Finn in a nightgown and frilly night cap, and tucked him into a big wicker cradle.

'Now, Finn,' she says, 'you'll be your own baby. Lie still and leave all to me. Suck your thumb so as you'll know what I want you to do.'

Finn did as he was told.

'Oh, and by the way,' she says, 'where does that bully of a giant keep all of his strength?'

Finn stuck his thumb in his mouth, then said, 'His strength is in the middle finger of his right hand. Without that finger he'd be as weak as a baby.'

With that they sat waiting for himself to come. And it was

not long before a giant fist pounded on the door.

Finn screwed his eyes shut, drew the blanket up around his nose, and tried to keep his teeth from chattering. Boldly Oona flung open the door – and there stood the mighty Cuchulain.

'Is this the house of Finn MacCool?' asks he.

'It is indeed,' says Oona, 'Come in and sit you down.'

Cuchulain took a seat and stared about him.

'That's a fine looking baby you have there, Mrs MacCool,' says he. 'Would his father be at home? I wonder.'

'Faith he's not,' says she. 'He went tearing down the mountain a few hours ago, said he was out to catch some pipsqueak called Cuchulain. Heaven help the poor man when my Finn lays hands on him; there won't be a hair or a toe-nail of him left.'

'I am Cuchulain himself,' says the visitor. 'And I've been on your husband's track this past year or more. Yet he's always hiding from me; for sure he can't be so very big and strong?'

'*You* are Cuchulain!' says Oona, scornful-like. 'Did you ever see my Finn?'

'Well, no. How could I? He always gives me the slip!'

'Gives you the slip, begorrah!' says she. 'Gives you the thrashing of your life, more likely. I mean you no ill, Sir, but if you take my advice you'll steer clear of him. He's as hard as rock and as swift as the wind. Which reminds me: would you do me a favour and turn the house around, the wind is on the turn.'

'*Turn the house around*?' stammered Cuchulain. 'Did my ears hear right?'

'For sure,' says Oona. 'That's what Finn does when the wind's in the east.'

Cuchulain stood up and went outside. He crooked the middle finger of his right hand three times, seized the house in his arms and turned it back to front.

When Finn felt the house turn, he pulled the blanket over his head and his teeth chattered all the more.

But Oona just nodded her thanks as if it was quite natural, and then asked another favour.

'With all this dry weather we're having,' says she, 'I'm clean out of water. Can you fill this jug for me?'

'And where will I fill it?' asks Cuchulain.

'Do you see that big rock on top of yonder hill? When we need water Finn lifts that rock and takes water from the spring underneath. Just as soon as you fetch some water I'll put the kettle on and make you a nice cup of tea. You'll need a cup or two if you're to escape the clutches of the mighty Finn.'

With a frown, Cuchulain took the jug and walked down the mountain and up yonder hill. When he arrived at the rock, he stood and scratched his head in wonder: it was at least as tall as himself and twice as wide. He held up his right hand, crooked the middle finger nine times, then took the rock in both brawny hands and heaved. With a mighty effort, he tore the rock out of the ground, and four hundred feet of solid rock below as well. And out gushed a stream that gurgled and roared down the hillside so loudly it made Finn shut his ears with both hands.

'Dear wife,' he cried, 'if that giant ever lays his hands on me, he'll crush every bone in my body.'

'Wisht man!' says Oona, 'he has to find you first.'

And she greeted the jug-bearer with a smile of thanks as he came through the door.

'Thank you kindly,' says she. 'Now take a seat while I put the kettle on.'

As soon as the kettle had boiled and the tea was poured, Oona set three cakes before Cuchulain – those with the iron griddles in.

All that work had made Cuchulain hungry. Smacking his lips, he picked up a cake and took a great bite out of it. Oh Musha! With a wild yell he spat out the cake and his two front teeth as well.

'What cake is this! It's hard as nails!'

'That's Finn's favourite cake,' says Oona. 'He's mighty partial to it; so is the baby in the cradle. Perhaps it's too hard-baked for a weakling like you. Here, try this one, it's a mite softer than the first.'

It certainly smelt appetising. This time he took an even bigger bite. But, oh musha! Again he spat it out with two more giant teeth.

'You can keep your cakes,' he shouted, 'or I'll have no teeth left.'

'God bless us!' exclaims Oona. 'There's no call to shout so loud and wake the baby up. It's not my fault your jaws are weak.'

Now, just at that moment, Finn sucked his thumb and guessed at once what Oona wanted him to do. Opening his mouth he let out the greatest, rip-roaring yell he'd ever made.

'YoooooowwwwllllllLLLLLLL…'

'Well, I be jiggered,' spluttered Cuchulain, his hair standing on end. 'What a pair of tonsil's that baby's got! Does it take after its father?'

'When his father gives a shout,' says Oona, 'you can hear him from here to Timbuktu!'

Cuchulain began to feel uneasy. Perhaps he was wrong to come in search of Finn MacCool. Glancing nervously towards the cradle, he saw the child was sucking its thumb again. 'He'll be crying for some cake any minute now,' says Oona. 'It's his feeding time.'

Just then, Finn began to howl, 'CAAA-AAAKKE!'

'Put that in your mouth,' says she. And she handed Finn a cake from the top shelf.

'How can a baby eat that?' said Cuchulain, scornfully.

But in the twinkling of an eye, Finn had eaten every crumb, then roared out again, 'CAAA-AAKKE!'

When the baby was well into its third cake, Cuchulain got up to go.

'I'm off now, Mrs MacCool,' he says. 'If that baby's anything like its dad, Finn'll be more than a match for me. 'Tis a bonny baby you have, ma'am.'

'If you're so fond of babies, come and have a closer look at this one,' says she.

And she took Cuchulain by the arm to guide him to the cradle, removing the blanket from Finn as she did so. Thereupon Finn kicked his legs in the air and yelled at the top of his voice.

'By golly, what a pair of legs he has on him!' gasped Cuchulain.

'You ought to have seen his father at that age,' says Oona. 'Why, he was out in the bogs wrestling with bulls at one year old.'

'Is that a fact?' sighed Cuchulain, eager to get away from the house before Finn returned.

'The baby's teeth are coming through well, though,' continues Oona. 'Have a feel of them.'

Thinking to please the woman before making his escape, Cuchulain put his fingers into the baby's mouth to feel its teeth.

And can you guess what happened?

When he pulled his fingers out, there were only four left: his middle finger had been bitten off.

You could have heard the yell from here to Venezuela!

Now that his strength was gone, the once mighty Cuchulain began to grow smaller and smaller, until he was no bigger than the cake he had bitten into. High above him Oona and Finn MacCool laughed and mocked the little man. The tiny figure tottered out of the house and down the mountain, fleeing for his life. And he was never seen again in Ireland.

As for Finn he was ever grateful for the brains of his dear wife, Oona.

VASILISSA THE FAIR

A merchant and his wife living in a certain country had an only daughter, the beautiful Vasilissa. When the child was eight years old the mother was seized with a fatal illness, but before she died she called Vasilissa to her side and, giving her a little doll, said 'Listen, dear daughter! Remember my last words. I am dying and bequeath to you now, together with a parent's blessing, this doll. Keep it always beside you, but show it to nobody; if at any time you are in trouble, give the doll some food and ask its advice.' Then the mother kissed her daughter, sighed deeply and died.

After his wife's death the merchant grieved for a long time, and next began to think whether he should not wed again. He was handsome and would have no difficulty in finding a bride; moreover, he was especially pleased with a certain little widow, no longer young, who possessed two daughters of about the same age as Vasilissa.

The widow was famous both as a good housekeeper and a good mother to her daughters, but when the merchant married her he quickly found she was unkind to his daughter. Vasilissa, being the chief beauty in the village, was on that account envied by her stepmother and her stepsisters. They found fault with her on every occasion, and tormented her with impossible tasks; thus, the poor girl suffered from the severity of her work and grew dark from exposure to wind and sun. Vasilissa endured all and became every day more beautiful; but the stepmother and her daughters who sat idle with folded hands, grew thin and almost lost their minds with spite. What supported Vasilissa? This. She received assistance from her doll; otherwise she could not have surmounted her daily difficulties.

Vasilissa, as a rule, kept a dainty morsel for her doll, and in the evening when everyone had gone to bed she would steal to her closet and regale her doll and say, 'Now, dear, eat and listen to my grief! Though I am living in my father's house, my life is joyless; a wicked stepmother makes me wretched; please direct my life and tell me what to do.'

The doll tasted the food and gave advice to the sorrowing child; and in the morning performed her work, so that Vasilissa could rest in the shade or pluck flowers; already the beds had been weeded, and the cabbages watered, and the water carried, and the stove heated. It was nice for Vasilissa to live with her doll.

Several years passed. Vasilissa grew up and the young men of the village sought her hand in marriage; but they never looked at the stepsisters. Growing more angry than ever, the stepmother answered Vasilissa's suitors thus; 'I will not let you have my youngest daughter before her sisters.' She dismissed the suitors and vented her spite on Vasilissa with harsh words and blows.

But it happened that the merchant was obliged to visit a neighbouring country, where he had business; and in the meanwhile the stepmother went to live in a house situated close to a thick forest. In the forest was a glade, in which stood a cottage and in the cottage lived Baba-Yaga, who admitted nobody to her cottage, and devoured people as if they were chickens. Having moved to the new house, the stepmother continually, on some pretext or other, sent the hated Vasilissa into the forest, but the girl always returned home safe and unharmed, because the doll directed her and took care she did not enter Baba-Yaga's cottage.

Spring arrived, and the stepmother assigned to each of the three girls an evening task; thus, she set one to make lace, a second to knit stockings, and Vasilissa to spin. One evening, having extinguished all of the lights in the house except one candle in the room where the girls sat to work, the stepmother went to bed. In a little while the candle needed attention, and one of the stepmother's daughters took the snuffers and, beginning to cut the wick, as if by accident, put out the light.

'What are we to do now?' said the girls. 'There is no light in the whole house and our tasks are unfinished; someone must run for a light to Baba-Yaga.'

'I can see my pins,' said the daughter who was making lace. 'I shall not go.'

'Neither shall I,' said the daughter who was knitting stockings, 'my needles are bright.'

'You must run for a light. Go to Baba-Yaga's,' they both cried, pushing Vasilissa from the room.

Vasilissa went to her closet, placed some supper ready for the doll, and said, 'Now, little doll, have something to eat and hear my trouble. They have sent me to Baba-Yaga's for a light, and she will eat me.'

'Do not be afraid!' answered the doll. 'Go on your errand, but take me with you. No harm will befall you while I am present.' Vasilissa placed the doll in her pocket, crossed herself and entered the thick forest, but she trembled.

Suddenly a horseman galloped past; he was white and dressed in white, his steed was white and had a white saddle and bridle. The morning light was appearing.

The girl went further and another horseman rode past; he was red and dressed in red and his steed was red. The sun rose.

Vasilissa walked all night and all day, but on the following evening she came out in a glade, where stood Baba-Yaga's cottage. The fence around the cottage was made of human bones, and on the fence were fixed human skulls with eyes. Instead of doorposts at the gate there were human legs; instead of bolts there were hands, instead of a lock there was a mouth with sharp teeth. Vasilissa grew pale with terror and stood as if transfixed. Suddenly another horseman rode up; he was black and dressed in black and upon a black horse; he sprang through Baba-Yaga's gates and vanished, as if he had been hurled into the earth. Night came on. But the darkness did not last long; the eyes in all the skulls on the fence lighted up, and at once it became as light throughout the glade as if it were midday. Vasilissa trembled with fear, and not knowing whither to run, she remained motionless.

Suddenly she heard a terrible noise. The trees cracked, the dry leaves rustled, and out of the forest Baba-Yaga appeared, riding in a mortar which she drove with a pestle, while she swept away traces of her progress with a broom. She came up to the gates and then stopped; then sniffing about her, cried, 'Phoo, phoo, I smell a Russian! Who is here?'

Vasilissa approached the old woman timidly and gave her a low bow; then she said, 'It is I, Granny! My stepsisters have sent me to you for a light.'

'Very well,' said Baba-Yaga, 'I know them. If you first of all live with me and do some work, then I will give you a light. If you refuse, I will eat you.' Then she turned to the gates and exclaimed, 'Strong bolts, unlock; wide gates, open!' The gates opened, and Baba-Yaga went out whistling. Vasilissa followed, and all again closed.

Having entered the room, the witch stretched herself, and said to Vasilissa, 'Hand me everything in the oven, I am hungry.' Vasilissa lit a torch from the skulls upon the fence and, drawing food from the oven, handed it to the witch. The meal would have been sufficient for ten men. Moreover, Vasilissa brought up from the cellar kvass, and honey, and beer and wine. The old woman ate and drank nearly everything. She left nothing for Vasilissa but some fragments, end-crusts of bread and tiny morsels of sucking-pig. Baba-Yaga lay down to sleep and said, 'When I go away tomorrow, take care that you clean the yard, sweep out the cottage, cook the dinner and get ready the linen. Then go to the cornbin, take a quarter of the wheat, and cleanse it from impurities. See that all is done! Otherwise I shall eat you.'

After giving these injunctions, Baba-Yaga began to snore. But Vasilissa placed the remains of the old woman's meal before her doll and, bursting into tears, said, 'Now, little doll, take some food and hear my grief. Baba-Yaga has set me a terrible task and has threatened to eat me if I fail in any way; help me!'

The doll answered, 'Have no fear, beautiful Vasilissa! Eat your supper, say your prayers and lie down to sleep; morning is wiser than evening.'

It was early when Vasilissa woke, but Baba-Yaga, who had already risen, was looking out of the window. Suddenly the lights from the eyes in the skulls was extinguished; then a pale horseman flashed by, and it was altogether daylight. Baba-Yaga went out and whistled; a mortar appeared before her with a pestle and hearth broom. A red horseman flashed by, and the sun rose. Then Baba-Yaga took her place in the mortar and went forth, driving herself with the pestle and sweeping away traces of herself with the broom.

Vasilissa remained alone and, eyeing Baba-Yaga's house, wondered at her wealth. The girl did not know which task to begin with. But when she looked she found that the work was already done: the doll had separated from the wheat the last grains of impurity.

'Oh my dear liberator,' said Vasilissa to the doll, 'you have rescued me from misfortune!'

'You only have to cook the dinner,' said the doll, climbing into Vasilissa's pocket. 'God help you to prepare it; then rest in peace!'

Towards evening Vasilissa laid the table and awaited Baba-Yaga's return. It became dusk and a black horseman flashed by the gates; it had grown altogether dark. But the eyes in the skulls shone and the trees cracked and the leaves rustled. Baba-Yaga came. Vasilissa met her. 'Is all done?' asked the witch. 'Look for yourself, Granny!'

Baba-Yaga examined everything and, vexed that she had no cause for anger, said, 'My true servants, my bosom friends, grind my wheat!' Three pairs of hands appeared, seized the wheat and bore it from sight.

Baba-Yaga ate to repletion, prepared for sleep and again gave an order to Vasilissa. 'Tomorrow repeat your task of today; in addition remove the poppies from the cornbin and cleanse them from earth, seed by seed; you see, someone has maliciously mixed earth with them!' Having spoken, the old woman turned to the wall and snored.

Vasilissa began to feed her doll, who said, as on the previous day, 'Pray to God and go to sleep; morning is wiser than evening; all will be done, dear Vasilissa!'

In the morning Baba-Yaga departed again in her mortar, and immediately Vasilissa and the doll set to work at their tasks. The old woman returned, observed everything and cried out, 'My faithful servants, my close friends, squeeze the oil from the poppies!' Three pairs of hands seized the poppies and bore them from sight. Baba-Yaga sat down to dine and Vasilissa stood silent.

'Why do you say nothing?' remarked the witch. 'You stand as if you were dumb.'

Timidly Vasilissa replied, 'If you would permit me, I would like to ask you a question.'

'Ask, but remember, not every question leads to good. You will learn much; you will soon grow old.'

'I only wish to ask you,' said the girl, 'about what I have seen. When I came to you a pale horseman dressed in white on a white horse overtook me. Who was he?'

'He is my clear day,' answered Baba-Yaga.

'Then another horseman, who was red and dressed in red, and who rode a red horse overtook me. Who was he?'

'He was my little red sun!' was the answer.

'But who was the black horseman who passed me at the gate, Granny?'

'He was my dark night; all three are my faithful servants.'

Vasilissa recalled the three pairs of hands, but was silent. 'Have you nothing more to ask?' said Baba-Yaga.

'I have, but you said, Granny, that I shall learn much as I grow older.'

'It is well,' answered the witch, 'that you have enquired only about things outside and not about anything here! I do not like my rubbish to be carried away, and I eat over-inquisitive people! Now I will ask you something. How did you succeed in performing the tasks which I set you?'

'My mother's blessing assisted,' answered Vasilissa.

'Depart, favoured daughter! I do not require people who have been blessed.' Baba-Yaga dragged Vasilissa out of the room and pushed her beyond the gate, took down from the fence a skull with burning eyes and, putting it on a stick, gave it to the girl and said, 'Take this light for your stepsisters; they sent you here for it.'

Vasilissa ran off, the skull giving her light, which only went out in the morning; and at last on the evening of the second day, she reached home.*

As she approached the gates she was on the point of throwing away the skull, for she thought that there would no longer be a need for a light at home. Then suddenly a hollow voice from the skull was heard to say, 'Do not cast me aside, but carry me to your stepmother.' Glancing at the house, and not seeing a light in any window, she decided to enter with the skull.

At first her stepmother and stepsisters met her with caresses, telling her that they had been without light from the moment of her departure; they could not strike a light in any way, and if anybody brought one from the neighbours, it went out directly it was carried into the room. 'Perhaps your light will last,' said the stepmother. When they carried the skull into the room its eyes shone brightly and looked continually at the stepmother and her daughters. All their efforts to hide themselves were vain; wherever they rushed they were ceaselessly pursued by the eyes, and before dawn had been burned to ashes, although Vasilissa was unharmed.

In the morning the girl buried the skull in the ground, locked up the house and visited the town, where she asked permission into the home of a certain old woman who was without kindred. Here she lived quietly and awaited her father.

KEVIN FARROW'S MINI-TALE

About two years ago, my granddad had not long died of cancer when, on a cold night on a Saturday, I went to bed at about 9 o'clock and about 4 o'clock in the morning I needed the toilet. I woke up and I couldn't move my legs. So I just thought it was my cat and then I tried to move again. I couldn't and then I saw my granddad at the end of my bed. All of a sudden he just went and I went to the toilet. When I came back, one of my teddies fell off the shelf and so I put it back on the shelf and it fell off again. Then I thought I'd just leave it. I went back to sleep and then I woke up again because I heard something fall over on the floor. I saw my granddad walking up and down in my bedroom, just smoking his cigar, and then he disappeared into my bedroom wall. The last night I saw him he came into my room, walked through the wall, and stroked my face saying, 'Go to sleep, go to sleep.'

*For the purposes of the first task on p126, stop the story here.